MATTHEW LAYS IT ON THE LINE!

Matthew
lays it on the line!

R. E. O. WHITE

THE SAINT ANDREW PRESS
EDINBURGH

First published in 1979 by
THE SAINT ANDREW PRESS
121 George Street, Edinburgh EH2 4YN

Copyright © R. E. O. White, 1979

ISBN 0 7152 0407 6

Printed and bound in Great Britain by
Morrison & Gibb Ltd, London and Edinburgh

These studies constitute in some measure the payment of a debt.

Recent research has thrown altogether new light on Matthew's Gospel, and in summarising its more positive results, omitting the technicalities, the present author is saying *Thank you* for some very refreshing hours.

If the result is to send many back to 'the Gospel of the Teaching', whether to confirm or to contradict what is here suggested, the writing and the reading will have been worth while. For they will discover how effectively, like 'every scribe who has been instructed for the kingdom of heaven', Matthew 'brings out of his treasure what is new and what is old'.

Contents

CHAPTER ONE

The quest before us

God gave us four Gospel accounts of Jesus: not one, nor two—'synoptic' and 'Johannine'—but Matthew's *and* Mark's *and* Luke's *and* John's. Yet with a strange perversity, reverent, well-meaning, yet destructive, we do our best to make them one. We strive to harmonise the accounts, to eliminate the differences, to deny outright the possibility of contradiction, to 'prove' with immense ingenuity that they all tell the *same* story.

Why, then, did God give us four?

For some purposes of comparative study, essential to balanced and fair interpretation, a 'Harmony of the Gospels' is necessary. But the chief result of detailed and exact comparison is to demonstrate how different *Matthew* is from *Mark*, and *Luke* from both. The writers share the same Christian faith, love the same divine Lord: but each sees Jesus with his own eyes, bears his own testimony, and frames his account for his own readers and their special situation. The inspiring Spirit who prompted the recording of the unique events upon which all salvation depends, did not destroy the individuality of the witnesses he had chosen, nor bid them slavishly copy each other. Properly appreciated, the divergent viewpoints only magnify the common message.

1

And to iron out the differences, as some ancient copyists and some modern interpreters strive to do, is to defeat the divine purpose in the diversity, and to miss the many-sidedness of the gospel of Christ.

The earliest known 'Harmony' was Tatian's, in the second century, the first of many attempts to construct a composite picture of Jesus. Indeed, for several centuries the New Testament began with 'The Gospel'—presented as 'according to Matthew', 'according to Mark', 'according to Luke', 'according to John'. Yet already *Matthew* was first, as most important, most authoritative, widely believed to be the earliest, and for most Christians *the* Gospel. It has been called the most important document of the Christian faith, the 'favourite' Gospel of the church. Certainly it was the most constantly used, unexpectedly so, remembering how Jewish it is in tone and argument, in language and appeal.

Moreover *Matthew* has retained its position all through the centuries. Not, indeed, as the earliest to be written: few students of the Gospels hold that opinion today, giving precedence to *Mark*. But for all that, *Matthew* is still held to be of supreme importance: for its massive presentation of the life and death of Jesus; for its invaluable preservation of the teaching of the Master; for its exposition of the meaning of discipleship and its usefulness as a manual of church discipline. Part of our purpose is to ask *why* this is so, what gives to *Matthew* its timeless relevance, even in our so different age and so very different world?

Behind this question must lie another: What gave *Matthew* its especial relevance to the age in which Matthew wrote? What did he have to say, or to show, that the others did not say, or had not made so clear? We may be sure that Matthew was not simply striving to be original; he would feel no pride in being merely different from the others. But we may be equally sure that when he insisted with eloquence and great earnestness on certain details of the story of Jesus, it was because he believed his own generation desperately needed to ponder them. Our quest, then, is to catch Matthew's personal viewpoint, to discern his mind and practical purpose, as he recalls his fellow-Christians to the memory of their Lord.

Inevitably, such a quest will involve a weighing of probabilities, the exercise of personal judgement about the precise shade of emphasis in this passage or that, about the intention behind certain omissions, or additions. We seek, with caution, the most plausible explanation of his telling of the story in the way he did and not in Mark's way, or Luke's— and that must involve occasional conjecture. We must therefore be careful, exceptionally careful, to keep close to what Matthew actually wrote. What we here seek to understand is his message to his own people: not what we can make each passage say to us, by distorting his words into the mould of modern questions to provide answers to problems Matthew never faced. To 'apply' what Matthew says to our own needs today is a separate, subsequent, stage in Bible study, not less important than the first, but not the same. Ours is mainly the primary task, that of seeking what Matthew was striving so earnestly to say to his own generation.

And so, though it calls for much patience, we must first familiarise ourselves with the Gospel as we now have it. We must examine, and summarise, attentively and receptively, what Matthew has chosen to say, before we begin to probe and to analyse in search of clues to the situation he was addressing, and the urgent needs he was attempting to meet. We begin therefore with the story as Matthew tells it; then we shall try to construct a skeletal outline to help us find our way about in his long and exceedingly rich narrative.

CHAPTER TWO

The story Matthew tells

Matthew introduces Jesus as the fulfilment of a long divine preparation, the culmination of messianic lineage, prophetic expectation, and an unmistakably supernatural birth. Some details of his infancy seem intended to recapitulate the Exodus experience of Israel, for he is hunted, exiled, and 'called out of Egypt as God's Son'. But in the visit of the magi, the wider world beyond Israel also pays tribute to him who is born King of the Jews and 'God with us'.

After an obscure childhood in Nazareth of Galilee, Jesus next appears among crowds who flock to hear a new reformer-prophet, John, who is preaching the imminence of Messiah to execute divine judgement, and calling for moral repentance, to be expressed in the purifying rite of baptism. Believing John to be 'from heaven' and to have 'come in the way of righteousness', Jesus is baptised, so identifying himself with John's mission.

At the moment of baptism, however, Jesus experiences a crucial vision, and hears the divine voice addressing him as messianic Son and Servant of the Lord, in language borrowed from Isaiah. He also receives the special endowment of the Spirit which had been promised to Messiah. In consequence, Jesus does not return to the domestic circle at Nazareth, but (still recalling Israel's Exodus experience) undergoes a solitary testing of faith and purpose, in which alternative methods of establishing the messianic kingdom are considered and rejected. Jesus returns from the wilderness having clearly identified the role of Messiah with that of the Servant of the Lord—a momentous step in his interpretation of his mission. Thereafter, Jesus found in the prophecies of the Servant (as Matthew shows) the pattern of his life and work.

Matthew then presents his portrait of the Messiah of *word* and *deed*. In a dozen verses he summarises Christ's ministry in Galilee, in fulfilment of prophecy, preaching the nearness of God's kingdom, calling individuals to become his disciples, and stirring immense interest and excitement by miracles of healing.

There the story pauses, as Matthew gathers into one discourse representative themes of Jesus' teaching as the Messiah of the *word*: the spiritual quality of those who enter the kingdom of heaven; the permanence and inviolability of the divine law to all who live under God's reign, and the real meaning of the law's familiar precepts; the demand that the people of the kingdom shall outdo all others in moral righteousness; the need to refine the customary forms of Jewish piety. Jesus calls for a devotion single-hearted and God-centred, trusting wholly in him who feeds and clothes the world of nature. Disciples must avoid censoriousness, while exercising discrimination; they must cultivate the life of prayer, live by the golden rule of love, and concentrate upon walking the lonely, demanding way to life. Jesus warns of false men and spurious

6

claims to godliness: only to have actually done the will of the Father will have any weight at the judgement. To hear and to obey this exposition of 'the higher righteousness' is to build life well, and securely.

Turning then to Messiah's *deeds*, Matthew swiftly reviews nine miracles of healing, so narrated as to emphasise Christ's power, the fulfilment of scripture, and the effect of faith. Attached to these stories are two further passages on the qualities of a disciple: the unhesitating trust that rides each storm; the mercy that welcomes even sinners in open friendship. Certain calumnies of the Pharisees against Jesus are then answered, concerning his alleged disobedience of Jewish hygiene laws, his neglect of fasting, his supposed reliance on the aid of demons. We are expressly told that such actions, teaching, and controversy, are but examples of a wide ministry conducted throughout Galilee.

Matthew then shows how this ministry of word and deed was shared also by the disciples; the calling, commissioning, and sending out of the Twelve is described in great detail, emphasising their full participation in his power, and in his reception by the people. News of this wide extension of Christ's influence in Galilee reaches John, now in prison, who had expected a different kind of Messiah. John sends to Jesus an enquiry which leads to a high tribute being paid by Jesus to the baptising prophet, and to a clear definition of the true relation of John to himself. Denouncing the inconsistency of Judaism in rejecting simultaneously two so different messengers leads Jesus to a general condemnation of the districts which, though highly privileged with opportunity, had rejected him; and to thanksgiving for the numerous simple, sincere hearts who nevertheless were finding the Father, and exchanging the burden of Jewish law for the easier yoke of Christ.

Two arguments about the sabbath then illustrate Christ's reinterpretation of the law by the principle of love. His meek, retiring, gentle spirit, while steadfastly reaffirming his purpose to establish the righteousness of God, only illustrates what Isaiah had foretold the Servant would be like. Further contention about Jesus' supposed demonic powers, and his refusal of the demand for 'signs', serve to underline how superior was the authority of Jesus to anything Judaism could offer. The outcome of the argument is a redefinition of discipleship as close kinship with Messiah, resting solely upon doing the divine will.

The perils that beset the work of the kingdom of God are next underlined, in a series of parables: the Sower, the Weeds, the Dragnet; the hiddenness of the kingdom until the end of the age is emphasised, though they who do find it discover wealth indeed. This parable-teaching, too, is shown to fulfil what prophets foretold.

Christ's sharpening conflict with Judaism is then explained: his rejection by his own home and family, and the public warning given to him by Herod's assassination of John, which made Jesus temporarily withdraw. But the picture of Christ is neatly balanced by the great story of the miraculous feeding of the five thousand and the stilling of the storm. In these two miracles, again, Christ is shown as the source of tremendous power to those who possess faith in him. Meanwhile, still as Messiah of the divine word, Jesus continues to offer to Judaism the true interpretation of her own law, this time concerning 'uncleanness'. This has implications for Jesus himself, and his mission among Gentiles: it is dealt with at some length in the story of the visit to Tyre and the interview with the Syro-Phoenician woman. The truth that emerges is that where faith exists, salvation comes.

Further contention with Judaism arises over the Jewish leaders' inability to discern signs of God's activity in their own time, and this is followed by a warning to disciples against Pharisaic influences.

Matthew then turns to Christ's purpose concerning the disciples and the church. The church is founded upon Peter as he confesses the messiahship of Jesus; authority is imparted, together with a call to share Christ's coming suffering. The story of the transfiguration of Jesus suggests the vision of the exalted Christ which the church carries in her heart; but the disciples' helplessness at the foot of the mountain suggests failure, through want of trust, to meet the needs of the world. The correct attitude of church members to the institutions of Judaism is urged, mainly 'not to give offence'; also to be desired is a continually meek and lowly spirit, combined with strong self-discipline. In any discipline of others, however, the church must ever remember her own debt to the compassionate seeking of the Shepherd-Saviour, and sustain an unremitting readiness to forgive the erring disciple.

A challenging and controversial question about divorce brings Jesus again to the right interpretation of the law and the meaning of being 'perfect' in respect to the law. This leads to further comment on the cost, and the rewards, of discipleship, although only the final assessment will show who is first, who is last, in the kingdom of God. This is illustrated in what is prophesied as about to happen to Jesus; and also in his reaction to an ambitious request, on behalf of two disciples, for foremost places in the kingdom: for Jesus also prophesies for them suffering to come, and states again what constitutes greatness in the kingdom of God.

A miraculous gift of sight, following public acclamation of Jesus as Messiah, leads fittingly to Jesus' royal entry to Jerusalem. His equally dramatic and courageous 'cleansing' of the Temple raises acutely the question of his authority compared with that of Judaism's 'authorities'. Jesus spells out a most solemn warning by publicly reinterpreting Isaiah's parable of the vineyard—a treasured affirmation of Jewish privilege—as only revealing Israel's barrenness, and her coming replacement by a new people as tenants of God's favoured soil.

The whole question of Jesus' authority is explored again as he is challenged concerning his attitude to Caesar, to scripture, to the essence of the law; and Jesus turns the tables on his questioners with a sharp enquiry about Jewish teaching concerning the true nature of messianic authority. In private again, Jesus replies to a question from the disciples with a discourse about the future: he foretells the rise of heresy, the spread of apostasy, and increasing persecution, before the coming of the messianic Son of man. Watchfulness is essential: both impatience and the certainty that Christ will return, demand it. Yet the advent of the Master-Bridegroom-Businessman will find many unprepared. At the end, though, divine judgement will sift sheep from goats, the righteous from those rejected by the King.

In his accounts of Christ's arrest and trial, Matthew emphasises the clear responsibility of the Jewish leaders. The disciples' unpreparedness and Peter's frailty are contrasted with Jesus' consistent and utter obedience to the law, and his initiative in all that happens. In the story of Jesus' death, his innocence is constantly underlined, while all conforms to the scriptural prophecies. Jewish charges that the disciples maliciously stole their Master's body are carefully related so as to anticipate the Christian answer: after a surprisingly brief account of Christ's resurrection, the falsehood of such 'explanations' is fully exposed.

Matthew's great work closes with Jesus exalted to all authority in heaven and on earth, commissioning his church to go into all the world, with himself—now clothed with risen power—always in their midst.

Such a summary begs many questions, and betrays serious assumptions that determine the selection of items to be mentioned, and the meaning assigned to them. Such questions and assumptions will occupy us fully as we proceed. There are special reasons, also to be examined later, why such a précis of *Matthew* should at places seem disconnected, even incoherent. But it will serve for the present to bring to mind the main course of Matthew's story. The overall impression is that of a massive argument for the kingship of Jesus, as Messiah of word and deed, the righteous Servant of the Lord, interpreting the law of God to men and accomplishing God's will in the world, only to suffer and die at the hands of unrighteous men; but he rose in might, and will yet appear in glory, when his kingdom shall be finally established.

A tentative outline

Skeletal outlines of Bible books can be very misleading. Usually they reveal more of the ingenuity of their authors than of the intention of the sacred writers, especially when symmetrical divisions and alliterative subtitles impose preconceived interpretations upon the text. Yet a careful outline that observes faithfully the pauses and paragraphs of the original writer can be useful too; it breaks up the material for study, and offers a 'bird's-eye view' of the whole, helping us to see where the argument leads, and how the separate parts contribute to the total impression and purpose. Nevertheless, the warning bears repeating: the outline can seriously mislead, unless we are extremely careful always to turn to the *book*, and not to the *outline*, to discover the author's meaning.

Attentive readers can scarcely miss the major divisions of the story which Matthew himself has provided for us at 4:17 and 16:21[1]:

From that time Jesus began to preach . . . the kingdom

[1] Numerous scripture references make for tedious reading. Where, as here, the exact verse is important, chapter and verse will be given; but in most cases it is sufficient to show the chapter where less familiar verses may be found (for example (5) means a verse to be found in chapter 5). An ordinary reference Bible will speedily show the parallel passages in other Gospels, where required.

From that time Jesus began to show . . . that he must suffer.

At once we have two greater sections, each with its dominant theme:

The Kingdom Proclaimed
The King must Suffer

and leading up to these, an introduction setting out the theme of the whole book (1:1–4:16).

Another phrase, repeated five times, is 'When Jesus had finished . . .', and it too appears to mark deliberate new beginnings (7:28, 11:1, 13:53, 19:1, 26:1). At three other points, and possibly more, Matthew appears to have paused to review and summarise the story so far.

Clear pauses appear at 4:23–25; 9:35–38. But 12:46–50 reads more like an interruption. At 14:34–36 a fairly extensive ministry to Gennesaret, with numerous miracles, is condensed into three summary verses. At 21:45–46 Matthew pauses to comment on the fears, and intentions, of Christ's enemies.

If we set down these natural, almost certainly intentional, breaks in the narrative, and ourselves summarise briefly what Matthew says from point to point, the structure of the Gospel comes to light:

Introduction: the coming of the King   (1:1–4:11)
Jesus' Davidic descent, divine birth, royal welcome and peril; his herald; his anointing at baptism; his testing

A: 'From that time . . .'—*THE KINGDOM PROCLAIMED*
(4:17)

1. *The Announcement of the Kingdom*   (4:12–7:28)
   Christ's impact upon Galilee; the kingdom preached; the
   fulfilment of the older law and piety in Christ's Sermon
   on the Mount

2. *The Miracles of the Kingdom*   (8:1–9:38)
   Leprosy cleansed, paralysis freed, fever stayed, storm
   stilled, demons expelled, forgiveness bestowed; mercy to
   sinners, and great joy; haemorrhage healed, death defied,
   blindness removed, the dumb made to speak: with a
   summary of 'the gospel of the kingdom'

3. *The Messengers of the Kingdom*   (10:1–42)
   Commissioned to Israel—the mission of the Twelve

4. *The King in Conflict*   (11:1–12:46)
   John's enquiry; the fickleness of people; the beginnings of
   rejection: criticism, accusations, demands for signs. Who
   is on Christ's side?

5. *Parables of the Kingdom*   (13:1–52)
   'The kingdom of heaven is like . . .'

6. *The Conflict Extends*   (13:53–16:12)
   Serious discussion—the fate of John; feeding the five
   thousand and its sequel; the claim to be Son of God, and
   further conflict; Jesus withdraws beyond Israel, yet
   crowds glorify the God of Israel; feeding the four
   thousand; a solemn warning of increasing opposition

7. *The King Recognised*   (16:13–20)
   At Caesarea Philippi, Peter for the rest confesses Jesus to
   be Messiah

B: 'From that time . . .'—*THE KING MUST SUFFER*   (16:21)

1. *The Sterner Gospel of the Kingdom*   (16:21–18:35)
   The cost of discipleship; the vision of transfiguration; a
   charge to secrecy; sad failure and repeated warning of his
   death; further demands and dangers of discipleship

2. *Controversies About the Kingdom*   (19:1–21:45)
   Concerning divorce, the law, riches, grace; new warnings
   of peril; cost of greatness; the King publicly hailed; the

14

entry to Jerusalem and cleansing of the Temple; his authority—Jesus accuses the leaders and warns that the Vineyard is in peril; the decision to destroy him

3. *Discourses Concerning the Kingdom*   (22:1–25:46)
   The great feast; Caesar, resurrection, the great commandment; Jesus denounces Jewry; the programme of the kingdom—the Bridesmaids, Talents, Sheep and Goats, parables

4. *The Death and Resurrection of the King*   (26:1–28:15)
   Preparation for burial, Passover; Gethsemane; Peter's denial; Jesus' arrest, trial, death, as King of the Jews. His resurrection

The royal commission: 'All authority . . . Go . . . I with you'
(28:16–28)

It would be foolish to imagine that Matthew began to write his Gospel with such a plan before him, or even in his mind. But that such an analysis is possible, without distorting what is written, is itself significant, and it offers already several clues to the message Matthew meant to convey. For example, the insistence that Jesus is King-Messiah, and that everything that happened to him may be interpreted in that light, is important. So is the amount of teaching, of controversy, and of reinterpretation of the law. But these and other details must emerge as we look more closely at *Matthew*. We shall not follow this outline step by step, but the passages we do examine should always be seen against its background, as integral parts of the whole, close-knit Gospel.

CHAPTER THREE

A closer look

Such a summary, and outline, of a book as long and as rich as Matthew's Gospel affords only a very general indication of his purpose. We must examine more closely, though still in a preliminary way, certain especially important passages, if we are to familiarise ourselves sufficiently with what Matthew wrote to be able to ask more searching, even speculative, questions about what he had in mind. At this stage, our selection of such 'especially important passages' must appear arbitrary: Why these, and not others? The answer, it is hoped, will become self-evident.

The introduction to Jesus
Matthew's very first verses exhibit his serious intention. The royal line of Judah is traced back to Abraham, father of all Israel, in three symmetrical steps of fourteen generations each, although here and there a name has to be omitted to achieve this pattern: Jesus' genealogy has been divinely prepared. Here is the perfection of providential design; here too, crowning all, is the supernatural birth, by the power of the Holy Spirit, of a pure virgin, in fulfilment of prophecy and the grandest of all Old Testament promises—'His name shall be called Emmanuel: God with us'.

The domestic and peasant welcome to Jesus that so fascinated Luke has no place in *Matthew*, but the king is troubled, Jerusalem is disturbed, magi from the distant east come seeking Jesus with regal gifts, ancient prophecies and a sign in heaven announce his birth, and an inspired dream protects him from imminent danger. Yet Jesus must flee for safety, as Israel once did, to Egypt's borders, as scripture foretold. Others bear the wrath of the king, and lament their lost children, as the prophets foresaw would happen. Eventually Jesus is brought again home to Nazareth, and another Old Testament text takes on new meaning.

Nothing is said of Jesus' boyhood and development; but in due course a new prophet appears—in fulfilment of prophecy—who announces Messiah's coming, prepares his way, and unexpectedly, on Jesus' own insistence, baptises him into public life with a divine acknowledgement and enduement for his personal assurance. Led of the Spirit now upon him into the wilderness to consider his future work, and ponder alternative methods of achieving his end, Jesus stoutly resists in God's name (and with God's Word) the allurements of the devil to seek a kingdom not of heaven; and he returns to Capernaum in Galilee, as the prophets had foretold. On the arrest of John, Jesus began to proclaim the kingdom, to call to repentance, and to gather about him a disciple-band. There Matthew pauses, to point out the great impact Jesus had made upon Galilee.

Providential preparation, royal context, prophetic foreknowledge, and messianic setting, all indicate something momentous going forward, a climax and a crisis in human affairs that is at the same time an

17

act of God on the plane of history. It is set within Israel but, as the magi show, it also embraces the world. Matthew is to tell of the appearance, at long last, of God's Messiah.

Two other details merit attention. It is interesting to notice in each Gospel the first words Jesus is reported to utter. In *Mark*, 'The time is fulfilled, the kingdom of God is at hand'; in *Luke*, 'How is it that you sought me, did you not know that I must be in my Father's house?' In *John*, 'What do you seek? Come, and see'. In *Matthew*, 'Suffer it to be so now, for thus it is fitting for us to fulfil all righteousness'. That, as we shall see, indicates from the outset Matthew's characteristic view of the purpose of Christ's coming: it is part of the message which Matthew underlines.

It can scarcely be accidental that in his introduction Matthew seems to stress a parallel between Jesus' personal experience and that of ancient Israel. Christ, so to speak, recapitulates the sacred story of the Exodus. 'Jesus' is the Greek 'Joshua'—'the Lord is salvation'. The flight to Egypt, and the record of Hosea 'Out of Egypt have I called my son', recall Israel's story exactly. Like Moses, Jesus escapes an infant massacre, and it is even said (by Paul) that Israel was baptised into Moses in the cloud and in the sea, showing that such a parallel is not too fanciful. Israel hungered, and wandered for forty years of testing, in their own wilderness, in preparation for God's purpose; as indeed Moses, too, had been tested in the desert, so was Jesus. The weeping of Rachel for her children, at Bethlehem, vividly recalls yet another crucial experience of Israel: the carrying of the people into exile. Each taken alone, these parallels might not appear convincing; together, in passages packed with Jewish, prophetic, and messianic thought, they suggest that from the beginning Jesus was identified with God's people—an idea that would powerfully attract Jewish hearts.

Much of the mind of Matthew is here already revealed, in the first few paragraphs.

The Sermon on the Mount
The famous 'mountain sermon' (as Matthew represents it) must occupy us repeatedly. At this point, we seek only to understand its drift and intention, in order not to misinterpret its separate themes. A further parallel is suggested between Moses' giving of the law on Mount Sinai and Matthew's arrangement of Christ's sayings, but it is altogether probable that some instruction was given to 'disciples' in the presence of 'multitudes' who overhear—the contrast between 'you' (disciples) and 'them' (the crowd, the Gentiles 5:47, 6:32) is carried through the 'Sermon'. Even so, more than the *four* disciples whose call Matthew has so far recorded seem to be intended.

We speak of Matthew's 'arrangement' of Christ's sayings because Luke also records about half of them, and it is of the highest significance that he sets several of the paragraphs of the 'Sermon' in very different contexts.

The Lord's Prayer, for example, according to Luke, was given when Jesus had been 'praying in a certain place, and when he ceased the disciples asked him, Lord, teach us to pray . . .' The beatitudes, and several related sayings, are in *Luke* 6 somewhat different in form and slightly different in situation from their setting in *Matthew*. The saying about salt is spoken to unthinking multitudes, in *Luke*; that about divorce, to Pharisees; that about agreeing with your adversary, on a quite different occasion; so are the warnings about heaping up treasure on earth, about the need of a clear eye to see the true light, about anxiety. The invitation to 'Ask . . . seek . . . knock' is part of a private conversation, in *Luke*, not part of a public sermon; and the call to enter the narrow way belongs to yet another incident.

It is possible, of course, that Jesus repeated himself endlessly on different occasions; it is much more probable, in view of the time that elapsed before any record was made, and in the light of other examples of Matthew's method, that Matthew has gathered into one 'discourse' sayings of the Master first spoken on various occasions, adding them to what was said on *this* occasion, and so presenting a clear, connected summary of the Master's teaching on discipleship. Luke preferred to record these sayings as they were spoken at different points in the story.

Seven references to the kingdom suggest that the King is stating the conditions of entry to the kingdom, and his laws for life within it. The opening paragraph (5:1–16) describes the kingdom-type of people: poor in spirit, hungering for righteousness, pure in heart, peacemakers, persecuted; how different they are, how happy, and how positive in their contribution to society! The supreme demand of life in the kingdom is a righteousness far superior to that of the scribes and Pharisees (5:20). That will involve, for scribes, a totally new interpretation of the law given 'by them of old time' concerning murder, adultery, oaths, retaliation, and enemies. It will involve, for Pharisees, a totally different motive, and a more sincere practice, in the traditional forms of Jewish piety: almsgiving, prayer, and fasting (6:1–18). The closing paragraph of the 'Sermon' (7:21–28) summarises the need for complete obedience to God's law (as Jesus now interprets it); only hearing and *doing* what Jesus says will render safe the house of life. This is the King's law, and the listeners comment upon its authority, compared with that of the scribes.

The passage 6:19–7:20, on the other hand, seems unrelated to the rest; and it changes the subject of discourse nine times! Reading carefully, it is possible to discern a list of alternatives which impose inescapable decisions: two kinds of treasure, two degrees of sight, two masters, two life-concerns, two gates, two ways, two qualities of tree; and Matthew seems to hear Jesus saying, 'Make up your mind, you cannot have both, or be both; do not judge others but do judge yourself—where you stand'. This is an attractive interpretation, though it over-simplifies by ignoring some details. Again it is *possible* that Jesus spoke in this disjointed manner, as well as repeating himself: but there seems little doubt that Matthew has gathered these isolated sayings of Jesus, also, and set them side by side within the 'Sermon', and we should read them so.

21

So Matthew portrays Jesus the King, issuing his law, as Messiah of the divine world and will.

The Messiah of miraculous deeds

Matthew turns from expounding Christ's teaching to displaying his marvellous power. Ten miracle stories follow in rapid succession (8, 9). The two brief interruptions are natural comments: the great excitement caused by miracles at Capernaum leads to warning against following Jesus for superficial reasons; and a miracle involving forgiveness of a sinner, set beside the call to discipleship of a tax-gatherer, leads to the affirmation that it was to call such back to God that Jesus came: the new spirit of the kingdom breaks through old *tabus*. Comments apart, each of the ten miracles exhibits some special feature:

The cleansing of a leper shows Jesus faithful to reasonable Jewish laws about uncleanness; the healing of a centurion's servant reveals unprecedented faith in a Gentile's heart; the raising of Peter's mother-in-law from fever is immediate, complete, and by a mere word, and seen to fulfil the prophecy about the Servant of the Lord; the stilling of the storm involves rebuke for disciples as well as for wind and waves; the healing of a madman at Gadara is not only duplicated (*two* men, to compensate for similar instances which Matthew omits?), but has an astonishing outcome: the *dismissal* of Jesus. Raising the paralytic demonstrates divine authority to forgive; healing the woman with haemorrhage reveals Christ's knowledge of the human heart, and his individualising gentleness; the raising of Jairus' daughter has about it the awe of resurrection. Two blind men accost Jesus in the street with a messianic title, but he waits until they are within the house before restoring their sight, charging them to silence. The exorcising of a demon from a man struck dumb leads to the crowd's acclamation—'Never was anything like this seen in Israel!'—and the exasperated retort of the Pharisees, 'He casts out demons by the prince of demons!'

Matthew himself emphasises that this is but a representative selection of the stories that could be told (8:16, 9:35); *Mark* has seven of them, but in quite different order.

It is plain that Matthew's choice was not made at random. Taken together, these miracles illustrate very clearly the grace of the King, the nature of the kingdom, the service of the Servant of the Lord, the power within his ministry; and the reason for his immense popularity in Galilee (see 9:35–38). But one thing above all others is here underlined, no less than seven times: the necessity, and the power, of faith: 'Your faith has saved you . . . Do you believe that I can? . . . So great faith . . .'; a chief lesson of the whole passage lies in the words, 'According to your faith be it done to you'.

The mission-charge
According to both Matthew and Luke, Jesus greatly extended his own ministry by sending out the Twelve, in pairs, through the towns and villages of Galilee to preach, to heal and to exorcise in his

name. Their brief instructions (as given by Luke) are greatly extended in *Matthew* (10) into a full discourse ending with the usual formula (11:1). To be precise, Matthew does not record their going out, their success or their return, but only their instructions. The same words are used to describe the disciples' ministry and the Master's; and this *sharing with Christ*—of his work, authority, vindication, rejection, calumny, secrets, acknowledgement, conflict, and reward, is the main theme of the discourse. As with the Sermon, so here parallels to certain of the sayings may be found scattered in *Mark* (3, 6, 13) and *Luke* (6, 12, 14), revealing that Matthew has again gathered them from different occasions to make one discourse, or 'mission-charge'.

But here an additional feature demands attention: of the charge's thirty-seven verses only twelve to fourteen apply to the situation in Palestine when Jesus sent out the Twelve (5–15/16, and 40–41). The rest, twenty-three or so verses, concern persecution by the synagogues, division of families, martyrdom, the conflict which Christ's coming created, testimony to kings, governors and to the Gentiles, and carrying the cross with Christ, which are all marks of the later experience of the church.

Up to *Matthew* 10 there has been no reference to Christ's being crucified; Jesus began to speak of that at 16:21. Thus, to speak of 'carrying the cross' at this point could mean little. During Christ's lifetime, no disciples were 'delivered up to councils, flogged in the synagogues, dragged before governors and kings to bear testimony before them and the Gentiles', there was only one governor in Palestine, Pilate, and one king, Herod, neither of whom arrested the disciples; while giving testimony to Gentiles in verse 18 contradicts the strict prohibition of this in verse 6. 'Brother delivering up brother, and the father his child, children rising against parents' and disciples 'hated of all men', Christ bringing a sword instead of peace—all this happened in later apostolic experience, but not during the days when Jesus chose and then sent out the Twelve in Galilee. There need be no question that Jesus warned of such things, but not in preparation for the Galilean mission, as Luke confirms (*Luke* 9:1–6).

Plainly, Matthew has again assembled what Jesus said, this time about sharing his work; and in so doing has borne in mind the experience of missionaries and martyrs down to his own time. In his account, Jesus speaks first to his immediate disciples in the contemporary situation in Galilee but also, so to speak, over their shoulders to all who would hereafter serve the kingdom (compare *John* 17:20).

Varied reactions to Jesus
In chapters 11 and 12, by illustrating men's various reactions to Jesus, Matthew tells how the Jews came to reject their Messiah, an explanation important to Christian apologists in Matthew's time. He records first an enquiry by the Baptist whether Jesus really is the expected Messiah, a question prompted by the unexpected nature of Jesus' ministry, carrying no

flail or axe or flame. Commenting, Jesus pays high tribute to John: 'He is Elijah, who was to come'; and then condemns the generation which, confronted by divine messengers so different as John and Jesus, could reject *both* at the same time. Sharp criticism of Jesus' attitude to the sabbath, and a plot to destroy him, lead to his withdrawal, on which Matthew quotes one of Isaiah's Servant-songs, describing the meekness and gentleness of the Servant of the Lord. Thus all happens precisely as the prophets foretold. Then Jesus warns against the 'unforgivable' sin of confusing him with Satan, and underlines the necessity of taking sides. For a crisis of judgement was upon the nation already: the only security—kinship with Messiah—lay in doing the will of the Father in heaven.

Inevitably, these chapters set forth also the signs given to that first generation, to lead them to the truth: the healing miracles, fulfilling prophecy before their eyes; the witness of scripture; the ministry of John; Jesus' other works of power; his fulfilment of the foretold character of the Servant of the Lord; his power over demons; and, greatest sign of all, Jesus himself: the 'sign of Jonah', that is, a prophet preaching (12:41). Similarly, scattered through the passage are the gospel's promises to those who receive Christ: happiness ('Blessed is he . . .'), the kingdom, revelation of the Father, rest, righteousness, hope, forgiveness, acknowledged kinship with Messiah.

But the dominant theme here is the variety of men's response to Jesus. John's question illustrates a sheer misunderstanding of Christ. The fickle crowds exemplify not knowing what you want of

Christ. Chorazin and Bethsaida manifest stubborn impenitence. The humble are perceptive and so understand, but others evade response by criticising. Some evade by violently blaspheming; yet others demand more proof, though no proof will ever persuade them. Still others, by refusing to surrender, are left more vulnerable than before to demonic evil. The overall message is clear: Christ forces himself upon no-one (11:15–21); but he will disown the disobedient in the end.

Secrets of the kingdom

In chapter 13 Matthew records three parables which in *Mark* and *Luke* are widely separated, and he adds four which only he preserved, so compiling a third great discourse. The kingdom is mentioned twelve times and 'secrets of the kingdom' is Christ's own title for this instruction, which will enable 'the scribe trained for the kingdom to bring out of his treasure things new and old'.

The parable method was familiar in Judaism, to make complex ideas more easily comprehensible, and abstract truth more concrete, picturesque, memorable, and life-related. Always it is necessary to ask what each parable meant *as Jesus spoke it* on the hillsides of Galilee or in the streets of Jerusalem. Thus the parable of the sower reflects, and explains, the experience of Jesus and the Twelve as the crowds began to dwindle in Galilee: only prepared soil yields fruit to God, even if the Sower be Christ himself. Limited, and even mixed results are to be expected: the sorting-out is best left to God's angels and God's time. But the power of growth in the kingdom-seed is phenomenal; the branches spread with wholly unforeseen vigour. Similarly, the leaven of the kingdom will eventually permeate the whole lump. Meanwhile, whoever discovers the kingdom finds what is of infinite value, whether in use (like treasure) or in its intrinsic beauty and joy (like a lovely jewel).

Matthew sees even in the *method* of the Master's teaching a fulfilment of prophecy (35): but his main thought in this discourse is of the immense privilege of the disciple, to know the secrets of the kingdom, which others do not know: 'Blessed are your eyes, for they see, your ears, for they hear . . .' Interpretation is given privately to those so privileged, just as elsewhere things hidden from the wise and prudent are revealed to babes. For spiritual perception is a fruit not of cleverness but of character, and of faith. To Matthew's readers, beset by unbelieving fellow-Jews, that offered great reassurance.

Christian relationships

Matthew's fourth great discourse collects together much of what Jesus said on the theme of rivalries and relationships among Christians within the fellowship of the church (18, ending with the expected formula at 19:1). Luke distributes similar teaching through his chapters 9, 18, 17, 15. The detailed procedure for settling quarrels within the church (verses 15–20)—as though Jesus was no longer with the Twelve—and the parable about the unforgiving spirit that may exist between 'fellow servants' of the same Lord, leave little doubt that Matthew again has in mind the later experience of the church as he records things the Master said about Christian relationships. Chapter 18 is, indeed, set within a whole section of the Gospel which is deeply concerned, as we shall see, with the life of the church.

Especially illuminating is the way Matthew adapts the parable of the Lost Sheep to a new use and a new audience. As Luke records it, the parable is part of Jesus' unanswerable reply to criticism by the Pharisees of his friendship with sinners (*Luke* 15). It is a defence of evangelism. As Matthew uses the parable, it becomes an argument for carefulness in dealing with immature fellow-believers within the fold, 'these little ones who believe in me . . . the brother who sins against you'. In Luke, the lost sheep is the sinner needing to be rescued from the consequences of his sin; in Matthew (if the whole passage has any coherence at all) the lost sheep is the erring church-member, to be brought back and forgiven—seventy times seven! It is expressly in such *use, adaptation and arrangement* of the church's memories of his Master's words, that we begin to perceive the problems Matthew faces, and the message he feels commissioned to bear to his own generation.

Last things

The fifth discourse assembles much that Jesus said about the future, and occupies chapters 24–25, with the closing formula in 26:1.

Popular belief about the future made much of the 'woes' that must fall upon the world as prelude to the end-time 'day of the Lord'. Some think that *Matthew* 23, with its seven woes pronounced upon the Jewish leaders, deliberately follows this pattern, and so belongs to the discussion of the last things. In that case, Matthew's fifth discourse is as long as the first, the Sermon on the Mount. But on the other hand, chapter 23 could be the close of the previous long debate, Christ's counter-attack upon the contentious authorities who tried to ensnare him.

If we include chapter 23, then Christ's picture of the future begins with severe moral criticism of misused opportunity and leadership: a foretaste, and a forecast, of divine judgement. For the rest of the discourse, it is once again clear that Matthew has brought together in one address sayings about the future which Mark and Luke assign to different points in the narrative.

Matthew 23:34–36 appears in *Luke* 11. Much of chapter 24 is paralleled in *Mark* 13 (though *Mark* (13:9–13) appears as part of Matthew's mission charge!) Some of *Matthew* 24 is recorded also in condensed form in *Luke* 21, 17, and 23. In chapter 25 the parables of the Bridesmaids, and of the Sheep and Goats, are preserved only by Matthew, but Luke has another version of the parable of the Talents. The same choices are still before us: *both* Matthew *and* Luke/Mark cannot be chronologically accurate in the setting of Christ's sayings; if Matthew tells it as it happened, then Luke has broken up the discourses and invented new settings for the sayings; if Luke is accurate in his settings, then Matthew has collected the sayings from different occasions to show Christ's teaching as a whole. The only other possibility, to evade this dilemma, is to suppose that Jesus continually repeated his sayings, irrespective of the time and situation.

Much that is most distinctive about Matthew's Gospel lies in his presentation of Christ's teaching about the 'End'—the 'last things' in God's programme of salvation. By the time Matthew wrote, the whole subject of Christ's coming and the end of the age had raised urgent problems for Christian thought and behaviour. Matthew is keenly aware of the questions being asked, and sets down with great care whatever Jesus had said that would throw light upon them. We have need, still, to examine with equal care the teaching he has preserved for us. Meanwhile, we notice only that the general effect of Matthew's presentation is to moderate Advent-excitement, while urging watchfulness, and *real* preparation by faithful service and obedient love.

The story of the Passion
The final section of *Matthew* turns again from teaching to action, the actions of Jesus and of his enemies, by which Jesus gave his life as Messiah and Servant of the Lord for the sake of God's kingdom and the salvation of men. *Matthew* is here largely paralleled in *Mark*, but such additions as there are carry deep significance. Matthew's account begins and ends with words of Jesus, and scattered through the story are twelve other explanatory comments which interpret what is going forward. Thus Matthew gives us Jesus' own explanation of his anointing, his entry to Jerusalem, his Supper with his men, and his death.

31

Throughout, God is shown to be in control of events. At point after point Matthew insists that the scripture is being fulfilled; Matthew *adds* that God 'attends' the crucifixion with miracles at the Temple, at the tombs of the saints, and in the resurrection. Jesus, moreover, goes voluntarily to die; all is said to be prepared, step by step: the Sanhedrin, the body of Jesus (by anointing), the betrayal, the last meal, the disciples, the Master himself (in Gethsemane). Christ's message to the owner of the upper room is 'My time is at hand'. He refuses to ask deliverance by legions of angels. Moreover, Matthew insists that Jesus died a *righteous* man, innocent of all crime; Judas laments 'I have betrayed innocent blood'; Pilate says 'I am innocent of this man's blood' (implying that there is guilt in killing him); the people say the same, 'His blood be upon us'; Pilate's wife sends saying 'Have nothing to do with this righteous man'. For the same reason, Matthew stresses that Jesus refused to swear an oath, to raise the sword, or to threaten the temple (Matthew says he was accused of saying 'I am *able* to destroy the Temple . . .'). Jesus *gave* His life, as the *righteous* Servant of the Lord; that is Matthew's view.

But the cross marks also the climax and the end of Jesus' humiliation, and meekness among men, as the Servant of the Lord. The resurrection marks the beginning of his exaltation and glory in the church, as the Lord to whom is given 'all authority in heaven and on earth'. In his story of Christ's passion, as everywhere in his Gospel, Matthew is saying strong, deep, important truths, which he would lay upon the conscience of Christians of his time, and of ours.

It was necessary to look thus closely and patiently at major passages in the Gospel, to attend to what Matthew says and how he says it, and to note his more obvious methods and emphases, lest in going on to ask more probing questions we should be tempted to read into the Gospel ideas the writer did not intend. Thus far, we have dealt only with preliminary questions, laying a foundation; yet already some of our suggested interpretations demand more cautious examination. Other suggestions, still to be made, will require even more scrupulous care not to misread what Matthew has written. It might be well, therefore, to pause here, and to read once again, if possible at one sitting, in any good modern translation, the Gospel itself. With its contents then freshly brought to mind, we shall proceed to ask, 'What was the situation Matthew faced, that prompted him to write the story of Jesus? What was the need that governed his selection of what to record, and how to express it? What exactly was Matthew so eager, and so anxious, to say?'

CHAPTER FOUR

Origins and consequences

The first principle of biblical interpretation is: 'What did the writer intend his readers to understand when first he wrote?' Granted that his words may well have a value and application beyond anything he could foresee; granted, too, that he writes—under the inspiration of the Spirit—truth deeper and more important than his own wisdom and experience; granted, again, that each later generation, reading what he wrote in the light of new problems and a new age, will find illumination and counsel that were not present to the writer's mind in precisely that form: granting all this gladly and gratefully, it remains true that the first principle controlling interpretation demands the discovery of what the writer intended to say. That is what he was led by the Spirit to write, and why.

The Spirit does not work by magic. When Paul wrote to Corinth, it was in direct response to *news* brought by Chloe's people and others, and to a *letter* which the church had sent to him. It is essential therefore to understand the situation and the church, before we can confidently understand the message Paul sent, and then proceed to ask what *that* message means for ourselves. The Spirit works, moreover, through individual personality, with all its variety of background, experience, talent, temperament, style, poetry, argument and appeal: nothing in conversion or inspiration irons out such differences. That is why Paul still writes like Paul, and not like Peter, or John, or Matthew; and why the same *words* in the work of two different writers, can mean quite different things; and why the first task of all Bible study is to see the sacred writer against his own background, using his own words, addressing the situation in which God placed him—and *listen to him*.

The first clues we seek to the circumstances in which Matthew wrote concern chiefly the kind of readers he addressed, and the sources of information within his reach.

The readers Matthew addressed
There are many indications that the expected readers were Jews. Matthew's constant use of Jewish terms and titles (binding and loosing, phylacteries, Pharisees, scribes, God's people, Abraham, Rachel, the bread of the Presence, these and many more); the assumed familiarity with Jewish ways and schools of thought (fasting, tithing, sacrificial worship, love of the Temple, and the sabbath, the festivals, the Pharisees' reputation for proselytism, are examples); the emphasis upon continuity with Israel's past, upon the permanence of the law, upon fulfilment of Old Testament prophecy; the whole presentation of Jesus as Son of David, Servant of the Lord, Messiah, interpreter of the Law; the appeal to the genealogy of Jesus and

the interest in 'the lost sheep of the house of Israel's
the adoption of rabbinic teaching method;
(mnemonic poetry using rhythms and thought-
parallels, and numerical arrangements of ideas—
Matthew sets twenty-four ideas in triplets like
almsgiving-prayer-fasting; Ask . . . Seek . . . Knock)
—all this, unexplained and quietly assumed, makes
clear that *Matthew* was written by a Jew and
primarily for Jews.

Yet the author is not pro-Jewish, or Judaist;
he does not defend the part played by Jews in the
tragedy of Jesus, nor does he seek to impose
Judaism again upon Christian hearts. His record of
Christ's criticism of the scribes and Pharisees rises,
towards the end, into a polemic. He recalls how John
insisted that the Jewish claim to be secure, as sons
of Abraham, was simple self-deceit; how relent-
lessly Jesus exposed the ostentatious and self-
righteous play-acting that passed for piety! how
Christ declared that Jewish tradition thwarted the
true law of God! how Jesus cleansed the Temple of
defilement, with stern warning to the authorities
as 'thieves'! how he once declared that he had not
found such faith in all Israel as he discovered in the
heart of one pagan!

Matthew recalls that Jesus once advised that since
the scribes and Pharisees sat on Moses' seat in the
synagogues, they must be respected when they
spoke in Moses' name, but their personal example
was to be abhorred: it is difficult to imagine a more
damaging criticism than that. The woes expected
at the end of the world all fall, not on the out-
rageously immoral and pagan, but on the religious
leaders of God's own people. The Sadducee

politicians are no better, understanding neither the scriptures nor the power of God; nor, as Jesus shows, the *ancient* faith of Israel, of which they boasted. Jerusalem the Holy City kills the prophets, and is fully responsible for destroying God's Messiah; in the end, Israel's elect privileges will be taken from her and given to others. It seems that *Matthew* is the most Jewish, and the most anti-Jewish, of the Gospels.

Yet alongside this trenchant criticism of official Jewry, every conceivable argument is urged why Jews should accept Jesus as Messiah, Servant of the Lord, and Saviour. The descent of Jesus from David and Abraham, and his birth in the royal and prophesied city of Bethlehem, his identification with the earliest experiences of Israel, are all meant to assault the deepest feelings of the Jew. The great Jewish titles are paraded—Son of man, King, Christ, Servant, the Chosen One, the Elect, the Righteous One, the Son, the Bridegroom, he that should come—to reverberate in Jewish ears. The Messiah of the divine word interprets the ancient law with prophetic power, as the people acknowledge; the Messiah of divine deeds is the vehicle of God's might, to heal, deliver and save: no mere miracle-worker and exorcist (there were plenty of them about) but one who in all his ways fulfilled the scripture portrait of the Servant-Messiah. All this builds a case that Jewish minds would find cogent and persuasive.

The one hundred and twenty-one Old Testament quotations are just so many arguments for Christianity, in Jewish ears; detail after detail in Jesus' story is *shown* to be in accord with the revered word of God. The whole of Matthew's representation of Messiah, from the circumstances of his birth, after preparation, through his baptism, ministry, transfiguration, death and resurrection, is authenticated by prophecy, vision, voice from heaven, miracle; and it might be shown how at point after point Matthew is answering well-known Jewish calumnies and misrepresentations. Matthew's Gospel is the finest, most forceful Christian apologetic ever devised for Jewish consciences.

This paradox—that Matthew as a Jew addresses Jews with both a severe criticism of Jewry *and* a moving appeal to Jews to become Christians— helps to define the situation behind the Gospel. When Matthew wrote it was still possible to win Jews for Christ; the breach with Judaism was not so complete or so bitter that conversions were out of the question. Nor do Christian Jews rejoice at what has happened to Jewry in the destruction of city, Temple and State, as they were to do later: in *Matthew*, the tragedy is described with horror. Nevertheless, the contention with Jewry as led by scribes and Pharisees is very sharp and increasing: there is no conciliation. Criticism, following that of Jesus, is still searching and forcible, and the accusation that the Jews 'destroyed' Jesus is still forthrightly levelled. At the same time, Jews already converted to Christ still need to be reassured that their new faith is true, is of God, and at one with the ancient revelation to the fathers.

There is one period in the developing relations between the church and Judaism which seems especially appropriate for just such a restatement of the Christian position as Matthew provides. In

Paul's day, Christian evangelism often began in the synagogue services, as at Antioch, Thessalonica, Corinth, and (so Suetonius says) Rome. But after two or three Sabbaths the Christian missionaries were ejected, often taking members of the synagogue with them. Sometimes, as a result, Jews took the lead in riots against the Christians, as at Ephesus and Corinth, and publicly repudiated all connection with the 'sect of the Nazarenes', so leaving Christianity without legal recognition in Rome's eyes. With the fall of Jerusalem (AD 70), and the steady increase of churches around the Mediterranean, Jewish hostility sharpened, and steps were taken to avoid Christian disturbance of the synagogue services, and to enforce Judaist discipline. The famous 'Birkath ha-Minim' edict introduced into the synagogue liturgy a new benediction in which Christians could not conscientiously join, so excluding them from Jewish worship.

While such an edict was in preparation, or at its publication (about AD 85), or perhaps as it was becoming known and acted upon in the following decade, such a book as Matthew's would have maximum relevance. It would be a time for the clarification of Christian claims; for a last strong effort to persuade fellow-Jews of the truth about Jesus; a time to expose the blindness and hypocrisy of the religious leaders of one generation which failed to recognise the Messiah, and to give another generation another chance; a time, moreover, to arm existing Jewish converts with telling arguments for use within their own circles, and to reassure those deeply shaken by the prospect of a final break with the faith of their childhood. All this Matthew does with consummate skill. He restates the case for Christianity in a way to serve convert and critic alike, by going back to Jesus Himself; *the Epistle to the Hebrews* is addressed to very much the same situation, but probably to some priestly circle, and uses more theological arguments to achieve the same end.

One possible small confirmation that this was the situation that Matthew addressed, lies in the way in which he speaks of the Jewish synagogue. Three times he just says 'the synagogue'; but six times he speaks of 'their' synagogue, or (to Jews) 'your' synagogue. Mark speaks like that in pagan Rome in a mainly Gentile church; Luke does so too, as a Gentile; but why should Matthew speak so, himself a Jew, unless because Christians were now being excluded? Further indications of the date of *Matthew* will be mentioned presently.

Where the Gospel was written is less important for understanding its message. From all the circumstances, in Palestine, almost certainly. Yet the ambivalent attitude to Jewry, the explanation of a few Jewish words, and of the custom of releasing a prisoner at Passover, may suggest the book belongs to the fringe of Palestine Jewry rather than to Judea. Since Ignatius, a later bishop of Antioch in north Palestine, seems to have known *Matthew* thoroughly and to echo its language, Antioch may well have been the Gospel's home-church.

The sources Matthew used
Our closer look at the contents of *Matthew* revealed

how much of what it has to tell is paralleled in *Mark* and in *Luke*. The similarities of substance, of language, and of order, are obvious even in English disguise; when comparisons are made in the original language, the facts which emerge are startling. Of *Mark*'s 661 verses, *Matthew* parallels no less than 600, and uses over half of *Mark*'s actual words; while *Matthew*'s order of recounting the various incidents in the story very closely resembles *Mark*'s, even where there is no intrinsic reason why it should. Where *Matthew* leaves *Mark*'s story to insert fresh information, a discourse or a parable which *Mark* does not preserve, we can see *Matthew* return afterwards to the passage it had left, and proceed from there.

Occasionally this is the cause of what now appears in *Matthew* as disjointedness; the story is simply returning to where it left *Mark*. It is of course possible that Mark was using *Matthew*, rather than Matthew using *Mark*, or even that both were using a third source, now lost, though that is merest guesswork. It is difficult to see why Mark, if he already possessed *Matthew*, should write at all; and if he did write, why he should omit so much of *Matthew*. It was not for the sake of abbreviation: his account of an incident which he shares with Matthew is often considerably longer. Moreover, *Mark* is full of vivid, dramatic, scenic and life-like detail: someone has counted 116 examples of this in the first six chapters. Mark too is more outspoken, one might almost say indiscreet, in what he says of Jesus' emotions, anger, ignorance (13:32), inability to work miracles,

41

and his denial of being 'good'. At such points we can actually watch Matthew toning down Mark's expressions to avoid misunderstanding: often we can see where Matthew has also improved Mark's language and grammar!

To compare both Gospels, verse by verse, in detail, is to be left with no reasonable doubt that Matthew is using Mark's Gospel as one source for his own work, borrowing, quoting, and improving whatever he needed to retell the story. Since Mark is generally thought to have written about AD 65–70, and time must be allowed for hand-written copies to circulate among the churches and come into Matthew's hands in Palestine, the suggestion that Matthew used *Mark* tends to support the date proposed for *Matthew*, around AD 85.

To rewrite and supplement *Mark* was an altogether worthwhile task, for Matthew had much more to record, especially of the teaching of Jesus. Of this additional information, Luke parallels well over 200 verses, and again content, language, and order are too closely similar for mere coincidence. Matthew and Luke seem to have had access to some source for the teaching of Jesus which *both* knew and could quote.

It is tempting to suppose that this source, like *Mark*, was a written document, now lost; but since we cannot watch Matthew using it (as we can with *Mark*) it must remain conjectural. Besides, non-literary societies develop prodigious memories. The whole system of Jewish education concentrated upon memorised passages: and

Christians loving the Master's words would have no difficulty in committing the great teaching to memory. Matthew and Luke *may* therefore be quoting what many Christians could recite.

Matthew has also some information about Jesus which no one else shares, some parables, incidents, and sayings which the church owes entirely to his diligence, and to his love for the memories of Jesus.

Luke tells us that 'many attempts' had been made to write the story of Jesus, not all of them satisfactory. Mark's is an all-important account, but mainly narrative, and composed for a mainly Gentile church at Rome. There was still need to supplement narrative with teaching, and to present the whole in a manner that Jews would find persuasive before the breach with Judaism became irrevocable. For that, Matthew was exceptionally qualified; and in executing the work he was inspired also to draw particular attention to certain teaching of Jesus which the church around him—in his judgement—sorely needed to remember.

Some illuminating consequences

Because we have *Mark*, we can watch where Matthew borrows, edits, improves, and occasionally omits; where he condenses and where he elaborates; where he rearranged into connected discourses and where he supplements with new information. We assume that he worked always with earnest and serious purpose. By what he selects or omits, emphasises, adds or occasionally repeats, we can discover with some confidence the issues about which he felt keenly, the problems of faith and of conduct that he and his fellow members of the church were confronting. As a craftsman of considerable skill, with the light of the Spirit in his mind and a great concern in his heart, Matthew—a leading teacher in the early Palestinian church by all the evidence—was doing what every Christian teacher, pastor, preacher in succeeding generations has felt bound to do. He retold the loved and familiar stories for purposes of exhortation and instruction, making new applications to new circumstances, using traditional material for contemporary purposes, showing the relevance of all that Jesus said and did to current needs, questions, and problems.

Exactly who Matthew was is not important for the understanding of the Gospel. The book is anonymous; the author evidently did not feel (as Paul, for example, might feel about his letters) that his own name would add anything to his argument. Ancient *tradition* that the apostle Matthew (Levi) wrote this Gospel, is based on something written by an early Christian—Papias —but unfortunately it is far from certain that he was writing about our Gospel of Matthew: some of his statements clearly do not fit this book. The apostle Matthew would be fairly old by about AD 85, and it would be surprising to find one of the Twelve needing to use others' accounts of the Master that he knew personally. The only contrary argument is that when *Matthew* tells (as *Luke* and *Mark* also do) of the call to discipleship of a tax gatherer, who then gave a feast for Jesus, *this* Gospel calls the man Matthew, not Levi. From the church tradition, it would seem that the apostle Matthew did write something, and his work may have been incorporated in *Matthew*; or the apostle Matthew may somehow stand behind the Gospel of *Matthew* in much the same way as Peter stands behind the Gospel of *Mark*. Who actually wrote *Matthew* is an unsolved but fascinating academic question; it is the *message* of Matthew that we seek.

Our study will proceed upon the firm opinion that Matthew—whoever he was—did use Mark's Gospel, and that where he differs from *Mark* he does so deliberately, and so reveals his pastoral intention. It is worth adding, though, that if we concluded otherwise, *the differences would still be there*; and Matthew's way of writing a wholly independent account would still reveal his own thinking, and purposes. In that case, however, our study would be far more speculative and psychological, for lack of evidence.

Thus, inevitably, something of Matthew, and of Matthew's own time, influences the retelling of the story. In one sense, the Gospel writers reflect two times: the *time of Jesus* in Galilee and Judea, and the meaning his words and deeds possessed for his contemporaries before the crucifixion; and the *time of writing*, with the meaning his words and deeds came to possess for the writer's contemporaries in their new situation after Pentecost. The Gospel writers are not pure historians, or research archivists, but pastors, evangelists, leaders in Christian communities: *they record what is relevant*, and do so in such a way as to make it forceful and effective.

But in Matthew's case, the more meticulously one studies the process, the more certain it becomes that Matthew remains faithful to the meanings and the implications already present in the church's earliest memories of Jesus. He may select, emphasise and apply; he does not *invent*. He updates the matchless teaching to meet the needs of his contemporaries: but he remains true to the Master's word.

A good example is the parable of the Bridesmaids. As Matthew tells it, the story ends with the exhortation, 'Watch therefore, for you know neither the day nor the hour'. The day, the hour—for what? *We* say, 'For the coming of the Lord': Christians should live in expectation of Christ's advent. That is Matthew's meaning. But when Jesus told the story in the streets of Jerusalem, *he was there in the flesh*, before the eyes of his own generation, among them already, and inviting them to the wedding-banquet of the kingdom of heaven. And most of *that* generation were unprepared, unable to read the signs of the times or to recognise their day of visitation. For them, it was not waiting but readiness that was needed; Jesus was not then talking of his second coming, but of the unpreparedness of his own generation for his presence among them, and for every approach of God. Fifty-five or sixty years later, as Matthew writes what Jesus had said, the application is again immediate—but to other hearers, in another time, about another coming.

It is this process we now go on to study. We watch how Matthew, towards the end of the first

46

century, *uses* the information that has come to him. We note what he selects to tell—and ask, 'Why?' What he adds—and ask, 'Why?' What proportion of space he gives to this story or to that discourse— and ask, 'Why?' By such means we hope to understand his mind, and to hear the message he felt impelled to preserve for his people, and for us.

CHAPTER FIVE

A manual for the Church

Foremost among Matthew's concerns, it is clear, was anxiety about the spiritual condition of the church he knew. He wrote for outsiders too; but it was the church which would take the message to them, and which needed to be armed for the work. And Matthew was far from satisfied that the church herself was ready to evangelise the Jews, or the world.

For centuries, Matthew's Gospel has been regarded as a manual for the church, and the reason is plain. There is more about the church in *Matthew* than in the other three Gospels together: about the church as Jesus intended it to be, and about the church as Matthew saw it, two generations later. Matthew believed that there was much that *his* church needed to learn about the church's beginnings, her nature, her task, and her future. Some have thought *Matthew* closely resembles the *Manual of Discipline* used by the Qumran Community of Jewish covenanters by the Dead Sea; others think the Gospel was intended from the first to be used in the church's worship (as we in fact do use it) for instruction, and discipline, of church life, expounding the faith and the rules of the Christian community. Neither suggestion is improbable.

The Church as Jesus intended it to be

The Gospel of Matthew is the only Gospel to use the word 'church' at all. We saw how in chapter 10 Matthew has woven around the original charge to the Twelve, as they went out upon the mission to Galilee, numerous other sayings and instructions describing the church's mission to the world, her experience of rejection, peril, and actual persecution, her sharing to the full in the Master's work, authority, experience, and reward. Such is the church's relation to the world around her: she is here to represent Christ and do the work of Christ; to be salt, light, a city set upon a hill, within society; to become a ferment within the mass of the populace: and to be Christ to her neighbours, as Luther suggested. Such is the church's function, to proclaim the kingdom of God, to heal and save, in the name of her Lord.

'Teaching, preaching, healing' is the description of Jesus' work in 4:23, 9:25, 'preaching, healing' is the mission of the Twelve in 10:1–7, and 'teaching' is added at 28:19.

In Matthew's arrangement, we hear of the church's function before we hear anything of her status and security, because she is essentially functional, a means to an end (in Matthew, a means to the kingdom) and not an end in herself. The church consists of people with a task rather than of people with a privilege; they are elect of God, as Israel had been, but that means elected to serve—not elected to enjoy being elected. Though Christ says, in Matthew, 'Come unto me . . .' it is the preliminary to 'Behold I send you forth'. Prior and fundamental to Matthew's whole thought of the church is the task to be done.

So the church is, in her essence, a mission. She is to bestow blessing freely, without charge, even as she received blessing without pay. She will sit lightly to all questions of property and reward, 'living off the land' like pilgrims and itinerant labourers, while accepting food from all people of goodwill, and co-operating with them. She will proclaim truth, and leave it to do its own work, without enforcement or resentment, knowing that divine judgement follows the rejection of truth. Since men do not like to be evangelised, hostility is to be expected, and cross-examination. Here the promise of the Spirit is first given, as especially the Spirit of *defence*, the Advocate of the accused, who shall equip the persecuted church to make adequate reply. Hostility will come still closer in divided families. Endurance is the saving quality: deliverance will surely come in time. In such ill-treatment, as in all else, the disciple shares the Master's experience. The great need is to have no fear, to preach the truth without intimidation, to believe in the Father's over-ruling care, and that in the end the faithful will be vindicated before the Father in heaven by the Son himself. For Christ will own in the courts of God all who own him in the courts of men. For a church on mission to expect peace and security is sheer misunderstanding: Christ brings a sword, division, and a cross, while the principle of discipleship lies in losing life to find it. But, when all is done, a divine reward awaits all who serve Christ's cause, even by so much as a cup of cold water.

Though in Galilee Jesus limited the disciples' mission to the lost sheep of the house of Israel, by the time Matthew has completed the 'mission charge' discourse, the wider world of kings, governors and Gentiles has been included in the function of the church. By Matthew's time the church was unequivocally universalist.

In chapter 16 the 'founding' of the church is narrated at some length. After several attempts to gain privacy to question the disciples, Jesus reaches Caesarea Philippi, and there enquires the reactions of the people to his ministry, and then the reaction of the Twelve. Speaking as usual for the rest, Peter declares that Jesus is the Christ, the Son of the living God. Immediately, Jesus speaks about the church, his own church, to be built expressly by himself on the rock of believing personality, on Peter and his faith, as Abraham, the father of the men of faith, was also called 'the rock'.

To the same believing personality is given at once the keys of the kingdom; for Matthew (as we shall see) thinks of the church as the way into the eventual kingdom of God. And with the keys, the authority to take decisions binding upon others. Moreover, the gates of Hades, the abode of the dead, shall not enclose or imprison the church, its members or its Lord—apparently a promise of undying life. This is a very great claim for the church: it is Christ's, his purpose and his accomplishment; it brings men to the kingdom; it needs not to fear death, for it will prove invincible. And its existence begins in and depends upon the open confession that Jesus is the Christ, the Son of God.

This is, in fact (as Paul in *Romans* 10, *Philippians* 2, and John in his first epistle, and other passages in the New Testament made abundantly clear), the basis of church membership throughout the apostolic age: 'If thou shalt confess with thy mouth that Jesus is Lord . . .'; 'Whosoever confesses that Jesus is the Christ . . .'.

Both Mark and Luke record the incident at Caesarea Philippi, but they have nothing like this high doctrine of the church. Matthew's considerable additions to *Mark* at this point indicate clearly the great importance Matthew attached to this theme.

In *Mark*, Peter's confession receives only the warning to be silent about Jesus' messiahship, followed by a stern rebuke. In *Matthew*, however, Peter receives a warm commendation and blessing, and then the great church-promise. The passage has problems, of course. The parallel with Abraham 'the rock', and the actual words of Jesus '*Thou* art . . .' make it probable that Jesus meant that Peter, personally, was the rock on which the church was founded, as the first publicly to confess Jesus Messiah. The dispute among the Twelve about who should be greatest may well have been occasioned by this gift of pre-eminence to Peter. That on the day of Pentecost Peter first preached the gospel to Jews, and in the house of Cornelius first preached it also to Gentiles (compare *Acts* 15:14 'first') may explain the privilege of the keys, though holding the keys of a household was generally the badge and responsibility of a steward, rather than a porter. For James, and not Peter, became 'head' of the church in her first years. Nothing at all is said here, of course, of any 'successor' to Peter—there cannot be any succession of 'firsts'. In chapter 18 the authority here given to Peter is given to the whole church (compare *John* 20:23). The words to Peter, like the procedure outlined in chapter 18, and the references earlier to teachers, prophets and miracle-workers within the church (5:19, 7:15–23) seem to assume for the church some institutionalised form, such as the church certainly possessed by Matthew's day.

In Matthew's fourth great discourse (chapter 18) we learn that entrance to the kingdom depends upon possession of the childlike spirit, while the discipline involved in 'entering into life' can be as costly as losing a hand or an eye. The church is charged to take especial care of the 'little ones who believe' in Christ. By verses 15–20, however, we are reading of the relations of quarrelling brethren within the *church*, of the rules for handling such situations, and for dealing with all joint church activities: deciding together, acting together, praying together, always with Christ 'in the midst'. The parable of the unforgiving hardness towards a brother of one himself forgiven (in *Matthew* only) is Christ's reply to 'How often shall I forgive?' though the exact truth expressed is that you must be forgiving if you have been forgiven, or wish to be.

In the background of the whole passage on mutual relations within the church lies Matthew's special use of the parable of the Shepherd seeking the lost sheep, set here as the pattern for the church's behaviour towards the erring member. Nothing elsewhere in the Gospels is quite like this detailed instruction on church-life following the account of the founding of the church in chapter 16. These two passages prove Matthew's deep interest in church problems, and his anxiety to apply remembered sayings of Jesus to their solution.

The whole church-setting of this discourse, with detailed instruction for church organisation, must raise the ancient question whether the hand, foot, or eye, of verses 8–9 were understood by Matthew to be (like the hand, foot, eye, in *1 Corinthians* 12:14–21) *church members* who offend the total Body of Christ. But this implies that Jesus commanded excommunication, and it is difficult to reconcile with Matthew's use of this saying in 5:29–30. The relation of church and kingdom must be further discussed (see p 99).

Matthew returns to the church's responsibilities towards 'young', weak and erring Christians: not to turn them away, cause them to stumble, or 'despise' them—no less than eight times, as any pastor might who finds his older, stricter members to be very unsympathetic towards struggling younger Christians.

In *Matthew* 26, the worship of the church is in the writer's mind as he describes the table-fellowship of the Twelve with the Lord at the Last Supper. Here is the central act of the church's life being established and authenticated by the story of Jesus and the disciples; though there is (in *Matthew*) no explicit command to continue the practice, it cannot be doubted that Matthew knew the church did so, and here recalls its historical foundation. The uniting bond of the church is the new covenant of Christ with each, and with all together: 'Drink of it—all of you'. The word 'covenant' recalls the conversation of God with Abraham, establishing Israel as the people of God; because of the chequered story of Israel under that covenant, forgiveness is central to the new covenant which Christ establishes by his blood. The sacrifice of Christ is as central to the new covenant as the sacrifice at Sinai was to the old, for at the heart of the whole idea is the thought of shared life, through shared blood. Further, Matthew emphasises the futuristic dimension of the Lord's Supper as a solemn and repeated promise of feasting with Christ in the kingdom of the Father that is still to come. Every worship-meal in Matthew's church is a foretaste of that final celebration. All this wealth of meaning is set, however, in Matthew's form of the record, within a sharp reminder that some are unworthy even now to sup with Christ, and will be shown to have been unworthy of the kingdom, on the last day.

In the closing verses of the Gospel, Matthew reiterates the commission of the church for all time, and does so in the most moving and heart-warming way. The church's central task is to make disciples. She is to do this by the twofold method, of *baptising* them 'into the name'—that is, into the possession—of the Father, the Son, and Spirit; and *teaching* them whatever Christ had commanded. 'Making disciples . . . baptising into the name . . .' recalls the basis of church membership already defined at

Caesarea Philippi; 'teaching them to observe all that I have commanded' recalls immediately Matthew's strong emphasis upon the teaching of Jesus and especially upon Christ's interpretation of God's law.

The scope of the church's task is 'to all nations', the limitation of the earlier mission charge is here not even mentioned, and finally superseded. The authority for the church's task is the authority now given to the risen Christ in heaven and on earth, shared, as the mission is shared, with Christ himself. And the abiding condition of the success of the task, the immeasurable resource for the church, is the continuing presence of the risen Lord, to the close of the age. That is Matthew's final definition of the church, and it cannot be excelled.

In view of *Matthew* 10, 16, 18, 26, and 28, it is surely not exaggeration to say that *Matthew* is the Gospel for the church. A few other references fill out the picture. The church of disciples constitute 'the free sons of God' (17:26), are 'entrusted with the mysteries of God' (13:11), have witnessed the fulfilment of God's purposes (13:16, 17). Matthew has more to say, too, about the church's relation to her Lord. But enough has been said to show how the thought of the church fills the Gospel, and how well he presents to Jews, shaken by any breach with the synagogue, the value of the divine fellowship to which they still belonged. The church has not been wrong in finding here the textbook and pattern of her life as Jesus intended it to be.

The Church as Matthew saw it
But Matthew's message to the church reflects not

only high idealism but sad experience. The church has proved to be a very mixed community, exhibiting all degrees of devotion, understanding, and faith. Once, through fresh fervour, unpopularity and persecution, the church had been pure in membership and steadfast in loyalty; by Matthew's time she consisted of many kinds of 'Christians', keen and faithful believers, adherents, enquirers, mere professors of the creed, 'little ones' whose faith needed fostering, hypocrites, hangers-on, critics, the disobedient, the unreliable, the useless, the quarrelsome and the unforgiving. Matthew draws attention to this *adulterated condition* of the church so often, in so varied ways, and always in memories of Jesus so deliberately added to Mark's account, that there is no room to doubt that this was the source of his anxiety, and one main reason for writing the Gospel at all.

The church is, for example, a field of wheat *and weeds*; a dragnet which has dredged up good fish and bad. Jesus had said, Matthew recalls, that this was how the *kingdom* would be, and as Matthew saw the kingdom in his own day, in the form of the church, the forecast was only too clearly justified. In the perfect, final kingdom of God, things will be different. Meanwhile (and the words should shock us still) 'an enemy' has sown weeds among the wheat: the explanation of the parable identifies the enemy as 'the devil' and the weeds as 'the sons of the evil one'—at work in the kingdom of God! It is useless, dangerous, and even presumptuous, to attempt to root out the weeds before God's harvest-time. That is work for angels, who will in God's own time gather the weeds in bundles and burn them 'at the close of the age'. *Then* will the kingdom of God be purged of 'all causes of sin and all evil-doers'; *then* the righteous 'will shine like the sun in the kingdom of their Father'.

In view of this surprising language, it can scarcely be questioned that Matthew understood Jesus to speak of the 'kingdom' (his word in 13:24) as in an intermediate stage, mixed, existing in tension, disappointing, marred by evil; and in an ultimate state, purified and glorious. The kingdom in its mixed, disappointing stage was the church as Matthew saw it: weeds and wheat together in the Lord's own field, all fish together in the gospel net, including some very fishy ones!

The Dragnet parable does not greatly vary the meaning, except to link the teaching with the ancient symbolism of the apostles as fishers of men and Christians as bearers of the fish-sign which spelled out 'Jesus Christ, Son of God, Saviour'. The Dragnet parable suggests perhaps more vividly how inevitable the sorting-out must be, with no mention of the need for delay.

Matthew shares the parable of the Mustard Seed with Mark and Luke, his only divergence being to omit the 'putting forth' of branches (*Mark*) and to say 'the birds of the air *come* and make nests . . .' Because of the position in which Matthew places this parable, between the story of the weeds and its explanation, it is tempting to ask if he regarded the 'coming' of the birds as an intrusion of creatures who have no true place within the kingdom, like the weeds and the bad fish. It is however far from clear that this was Matthew's intention.

Only Matthew has the parables of Weeds and Dragnet, which he did not preserve without some strong purpose. But their teaching is everywhere in his Gospel, as he recalls saying after saying, and numerous incidents, which make the same point. Even around the Lord's Table there are those who must beware of betraying Christ, who need to ask 'Is it I?' and the Master himself draws attention to the fact (26:21, 23, and 31). There were, on the hill above Bethany, even around the risen Lord, some who doubted. Why *does* Matthew add that curt phrase at such a moment? Many call Jesus 'Lord, Lord . . .' (in baptism?) and do not the things he says. Among the guests at Messiah's banquet are some without wedding garments: they wear cast-offs, and must eventually be cast out. Even among the bridesmaids sharing the Bridegroom's wedding, there are some very foolish girls. In the congregation who listen and *hear* Christ's words are some who are wise to build their lives according to what they know, but others who also hear, and know, yet build their lives differently: some wise and some foolish *students of the Word*.

There are ten-talent church members, gifted and busy; there are five-talent members, less gifted, but equally busy; there are others neither gifted nor busy: lazy and profitless. In the very flock of the good Shepherd there are in fact sheep *and goats*. One son says, in response to the evangelical appeal, 'I go sir' but does not go; another refuses 'No, I will not', but he goes. 'Many are called' (Matthew's church congregation seems to have been large) 'but few are chosen'.

But also—still recalling words of Jesus—'many fall

away . . .'; they betray one another, even 'hate' one another; false teachers lead others astray to new sects and movements; because wickedness is multiplied, the love of *most* grows cold. Some *servants of the Lord* have become faithless, drunken, given to beating their fellow-servants. Matthew seems to live among backsliders.

It will be necessary to examine carefully the causes of Matthew's concern and the precise weaknesses to which he draws most attention. Whatever these prove to be, Matthew believed that the Master had said and done things directly relevant to such deficiencies; that if only the church knew her Lord better such faults would disappear from her life. That is why he goes back to Jesus, writing a Gospel rather than an epistle or treatise. He considered that the church of his own day needed to hear again the Master's plain speaking on Christian ethics, Christian work, and Christian resources, and he was determined that the mixed, half-nominal, backsliding community which he knew should no longer have the excuse of ignorance. Matthew's bent of mind was pre-eminently practical, and no-one was more practical than Jesus: so Matthew demands that we listen to the Master, and find in his matchless words the antidote to all the church's ills.

CHAPTER SIX

For a Church
ethically confused

It is neither pastorally wise nor psychologically sound to concentrate upon fault and failure. Matthew's indictment of the church was severe and negative enough: wild weeds, worthless fish, causes of sin, love growing cold. But that charge does not express the urgency of Matthew's concern. He was not merely disappointed that some Christians whom he knew were not as committed to Christ as they might have been. He was contending against something far more serious. He considered that the church of Christ had become ethically confused, morally astray from the gospel.

We know that versions of Christianity had arisen in which orthodoxy of belief, or intensity of emotional experience, pride of spiritual knowledge, even confidence in some link with the Christian pioneers, had come to possess supreme importance, instead of a transformed character and holiness of life. Matthew was aware of this. There were those who thought that personal goodness, simple rectitude of conduct, purity of heart, truthfulness of speech, fairness of mind, uprightness and kindliness, have little to do with religious experience. There were even those, Matthew recalls that Jesus said so, who not only relax the commandments of

God for themselves but who teach others to do so too, causing them to stumble in the Christian way.

To Matthew's mind, this was a gross misrepresentation of the Master and of the gospel, and the root cause of the sad condition of the church. Christians seemed to have forgotten that the highest end of all their faith, experience, and profession is *right living*. In Matthew's opinion, they needed nothing more desperately than a strong reminder of the moral teaching of Jesus. In recalling that teaching, deliberately and faithfully, Matthew refers to righteousness, or to righteous judgement, thirty-five times in twenty-eight chapters.

Matthew on righteousness

Just who were these 'false prophets' who denigrated ethical instruction among Christians and disparaged righteousness, is not clear. They may not be an identifiable group within the church; it is possible they represent a constant tendency within evangelical Christianity itself.

Matthew knows that the Pharisees, for the sake of their tradition, made void the word (or law) of God (15:6). The Qumran covenanters accused the rabbis and the scribes of diluting God's law, 'teaching smooth things'. But Matthew's insistence upon righteousness is addressed mainly to his Christian readers. It seems that some were saying, 'the law and the prophets were until John', implying that since John, Christ had abrogated the old demands for right living; for Matthew carefully changes this to 'the law and the prophets *prophesied* until John', so avoiding the implication that the law was no longer valid.

In Paul's day, 'Judaisers' attempted to enforce Jewish rules concerning the sabbath, circumcision, and unclean foods, upon Gentile believers; and Paul strenuously opposed this, declaring that 'Christ is the end of the law'. But there is no evidence that Matthew has Paul in mind, or that this controversy still troubled the church in Matthew's day; these specific issues as they affected Gentile Christians are not discussed in *Matthew*.

It seems most probable that Matthew has in mind any who pretend that righteousness does not matter for Christians. Some who did this were merely seeking to emphasise that God freely forgives the sinner who has no works or merit to offer in atonement for his sins. For the truly penitent, their lack of righteousness is no bar to the pardon of God. Others, however, believed that given true faith, a saving experience of the grace of God, all questions of morality, obedience and righteousness looked after themselves; all attention given to ethical issues called in question the transforming power of God, and involved a fall from the level of grace. Others again appear to have argued that since 'where sin increased, grace abounded all the more' it is actually possible to continue in sin that grace may abound still more! (*Romans* 5:20, 6:1).

Matthew's answer is forthright, and disconcerting. He takes up a saying of Jesus which no-one else preserves, and lays it squarely upon the conscience of the church:

'I tell you, unless your righteousness exceeds that

*of the scribes and Pharisees, you will never enter
the kingdom of heaven.'* (5:20)

That is surely unanswerable.

Admittedly, 'righteous' and 'righteousness' are
not words that we like. They do not spring readily to
mind when we think of the moral fruits of the gospel.
We prefer to speak in warmer language, about the
goodness of fine people, about the *value* of behaving
well. But to a Jew, and so to Matthew, this way of
speaking is not enough, for two reasons: First,
because it defines moral conduct as something *we*
happen to approve; secondly, because it bases
approval upon what is considered good, or profit-
able, for us or for society; what has value in
promoting human welfare. The Jewish view, and
later the Christian view, held that moral conduct
consists of what is *right*, irrespective of any good, or
value, by which it might be rewarded; and irrespective, too, of any loss by sacrifice or persecution
which moral conduct might cost us. Even more
important, the Jewish-Christian view insisted that
moral conduct consists in what is *right in the sight of
the Lord*. The standard was not human assessment
but divine law.

And that is precisely what 'righteousness' implies. It is a way of living assessed strictly by its
ethical quality, and not first by its individual or social
expediency. It is measured by an objective, divine
standard, and not by a human one. For Matthew,
righteousness means the character, the conduct,
which is right with God, right according to God's
judgement law, and commandments (as Matthew
says so often). Much will depend of course upon

what we include in 'righteousness'. We cannot ignore the consequences of what we do, and consider something 'right' however much it hurts others. Nor can we depend entirely upon some written rule and apply it rigidly in all circumstances; Matthew will strongly contend that careful criticism of traditional views of divine law is essential to 'righteousness'.

Moreover, in Christian circles the word has gained a bad odour, as phrases like 'mere righteousness', 'self-righteousness', 'law-righteousness', and even 'filthy-rags righteousness' sufficiently show, and there are reasons for this attitude. Nevertheless, for every Jew, including Matthew, righteousness was the paramount aim of all godliness, and to have one's *rightness* of heart, and *rightness* of conduct, accepted by God and vindicated before men was to the pious in Israel the highest attainable bliss.

There is a translation problem here. Sometimes righteousness is required especially in social relationships, but then the same root-idea is translated *justice*; and *to do justly* was the first of the requirements of God even to a prophet, as to Micah. So, too, according to the psalmists the true man of God is the *righteous* or *just* man. Sometimes, again, the desire to be approved by God, to be counted righteous in the supreme court of heaven, is called '*being justified*'.

In practice, righteousness of life consisted in conforming to the divine will as revealed in the Law. He who does 'what is lawful and right . . . walking in my statutes, careful to observe my ordinances, he is righteous' (*Ezekiel* 18:5–9). This meant also being conformed with the divine character: for the righteousness of God himself was the source of the righteousness of the Law. In this way, to the Hebrew mind, 'righteousness' always implied God-likeness.

Later, God showed his righteousness toward Israel by delivering her from foreign oppression; and so God's righteousness came to signify deliverance or salvation, as often in Isaiah. Further, God's delivering righteousness was especially promised to defend the poor and oppressed 'saints', and 'righteousness' came to approximate to 'caring for people as God cares'. In *Matthew* 6:2 some important ancient copies actually have 'righteousness' for almsgiving.

All this inherited breadth of thought lies within Matthew's insistence that the disciple of Jesus must seek the kingdom of God *and his righteousness*.

Paul expresses the supreme aim of religion in precisely this way. Still within Judaism, it was his boast that he was 'as to the righteousness under the law, blameless'; later, in Christ, it is still God's will that 'the just requirement of the law might be fulfilled in us'. That all men failed, in practice, to attain to righteousness, was the problem to which the gospel of Christ was addressed: Christianity solved it, not by abrogating the demand but by attaining it another way —through the Spirit of life in Christ Jesus (*Romans* 8:1–4; compare *1 Corinthians* 6:9).

To appreciate the full force of Matthew's argument, however, we must look a little further through the New Testament. One of Paul's metaphors for salvation was this very same idea of *becoming righteous* in God's sight. In plain fact no man deserved to be: all were *guilty* before God. But in the gospel those who believed in Christ were accounted righteous (justified) through their faith. Once Paul declares that Christ is made unto us righteousness; usually it is faith that is counted for righteousness, as it was for Abraham—as Paul says, 'not . . . a righteousness of my own, based on law, but that which is through faith in Christ, the righteousness from God that depends on faith'. So 'the just (righteous) shall live by faith' and not by works of righteousness which he has done.

This is of course the only hope of acceptance with God open to the sinner, who has no righteousness of his own to offer. But this formulation of the gospel had led in the early church to a certain misunderstanding, and to some difficulty with younger Christians. James, for example, felt it necessary to insist that when faith is reckoned as righteousness, very much depends upon what you mean by faith: for *even the demons have faith* and are afraid, not justified. John in his epistle roundly declared, 'Little children, let no one deceive you. *He who does right* is righteous, as he is righteous'. Matthew is making the same protest. It must not be imagined (he insists) that because the sinner is forgiven—that is, treated as righteous, as though he had not sinned—that therefore he does not need to *become* righteous in character and conduct. Christ did indeed come 'not to call the righteous, but sinners': but to call them to righteousness.

In the life and character of the church around him,

Matthew saw the consequences of that grave misunderstanding. That is why he lays down with the authority of Jesus his relentless, absolute, and forbidding rule:

> *Unless your righteousness exceeds that of the scribes and Pharisees, you will never enter the kingdom of heaven*

and elaborates it with over thirty other references. But Matthew goes further: he defines the whole work of Christ as the establishing of righteousness; and the essence of discipleship, in consequence, as a search for righteousness.

Christ and righteousness
Jesus' first utterance in *Matthew*, 'It is fitting for us to fulfil all righteousness', sets the keynote for his ministry. The programme so announced is summarised by Matthew in words of Isaiah:

> 'Behold, my servant whom I have chosen,
>   my beloved with whom my soul is well pleased.
> I will put my Spirit upon him,
>   and he shall proclaim justice to the Gentiles.
> He will not wrangle or cry aloud,
>   nor will any one hear his voice in the streets;
> he will not break a bruised reed
>   or quench a smouldering wick,
> till he brings justice to victory;
>   and in his name will the Gentiles hope'

and Matthew declares that Jesus matched perfectly this portrait of the Servant of the Lord. Two details are especially significant. 'To proclaim justice', 'to bring justice to victory', is here a ground of *hope*;

this 'justice' is evidently not divine judgement to be feared but the establishing of divine righteousness in an unjust world. That is always the hope of the oppressed, the ill-used, the persecuted, in all generations. Equally significant is Matthew's addition of the phrase 'to victory'. The words are not in *Isaiah* 42; Matthew inserted them to define more clearly the work of the Servant as he understood it: to make God's righteousness *triumph* in the earth.

In the beginning, immediately following the baptismal announcement of this purpose, Matthew shows (unlike Mark) that angels ministered to Jesus *when he had overcome the devil* by asserting God's will. At the end Jesus dies a righteous man, amid repeated testimonies to his innocence and avoiding even the appearance of evil. Matthew insists that Jesus died voluntarily, in submission to the divine will; being 'delivered up' he 'must suffer' when his 'time is at hand'. His prayer, 'Father, if this cannot pass unless I drink it, thy will be done' expresses the perfect obedience to divine command in which, for Matthew, righteousness consists. So, dying in righteousness, Jesus looks for immediate vindication (23:39, 26:64—literally, 'from now').

This (as we saw) is Matthew's account of the passion, emphasising that Christ's death was all part of the righteous will of God, as prophecy defined it, and as God's interventions at the time clearly demonstrated. 'The Righteous One' (as Peter at Pentecost and John in his epistle describe Jesus), 'my righteous servant' (in Isaiah's words), the teacher of righteousness, having fulfilled all righteousness throughout his life, brought God's righteous judgement to victory by his death. For that

death, by establishing the divine kingdom in count-
less redeemed hearts, did not defeat God's will, but
wonderfully achieved it among men; just as Christ's
own grace, forgivingness, and submission in death,
showed how completely the will of God ruled within
himself. That was the Servant-Messiah's work:
establishing on earth a kingdom of righteous men,
under the righteous God, by a willing death which
fulfilled the righteous will of God.

This interpretation of Messiah's work was not
entirely new. The rabbis held that the messianic
age would see the divine law fulfilled, and taught
in pagan theatres and circuses. The evil impulse
would be purged from all hearts, and all Israel
would keep the law. Messiah himself would study
the law and explain it. Some of the popular
apocalyptic writers, too, held that in the days of
Messiah the righteous one, righteousness would
reign, Jerusalem would be holy, all wickedness
would be done away. Messiah would teach
righteousness and destroy sinners. Isaiah has
fifteen distinct prophecies that Messiah will
establish God's justice and righteousness in the
earth. The Dead Sea Scrolls show that the hero of
the Qumran community was 'the teacher of
righteousness'.

Matthew's portrait of the righteous Messiah
executing God's righteous will on earth is plainly in
line with the highest Jewish expectations—a
persuasive argument, both for his opponents and
for his fellow Jewish-Christians.

Disciples and righteousness

It follows that disciples must seek the kingdom of God *and his righteousness*; must hunger and thirst *after righteousness*; must be willing to suffer *for righteousness' sake*; must so prepare that in the end, at the judgement, separated from all that defiles, they will shine as the sun in the kingdom of the Father *as the righteous*. For to enter the kingdom at all demands 'exceeding' righteousness (5:20). By that startling saying, the necessity for righteousness in the life of a disciple is placed beyond all question. We must outdo the Pharisees in striving after righteousness—or stay outside the kingdom!

The final charge to disciples is to teach 'whatever I have commanded', for the righteousness which marked the devout of the old covenant—strict obedience to divine commandments—must distinguish equally their successors (13:17, 23:29, 10:41), the coming generations of disciples, to the end of the age.

That is why Matthew recalls, repeatedly, those trenchant warnings of Jesus against *self-deception* in this matter of discipleship. 'Many that are first shall be last'—that was the reply of Jesus to the over-confident Peter, so sure of a prominent place in the kingdom because he had given up so much. But the words occur again in *Matthew*—always a significant sign of emphasis—as a deliberate comment upon the workers in the vineyard who persuaded themselves that they deserved a greater reward than others (19:30, 20:16). The words can only mean that many who think themselves first will find that they are last.

The one-talent servant, who thought his master a hard man and so feared failure that he did nothing with his talent, was playing for safety; he was therefore the more astonished to find himself thrust out of the master's household into darkness and the idleness of the streets. There could never be security, in the service of such a one as Jesus, in merely avoiding risk! In the same way, the guest who succeeded, somehow, in getting to the wedding feast unfittingly attired, was left 'speechless' when his presence was challenged: he was so sure of his right to the favours of his host. Many evangelicals are still shocked to hear Jesus speak, with triple emphasis, of those who think themselves disciples but are 'not worthy of me—not worthy of me—not worthy of me' (10:34–38). Is not Christian discipleship a gift of divine grace, irrespective of all 'worthiness'? Jesus' reply to all presumptuous over-confidence is the incisive admonition: 'Many are called, but few are chosen'.

And the danger is spelled out in detail. Some ostensible disciples rely upon persistent and emphatic professions of faith—'Lord, Lord'—as sufficient evidence of their standing with Christ. If we are right to link this expression (7:21) with the profession of faith in Christ required at baptism as the basis of church membership, then the warning is directed especially against a formal and ritual church-membership which subscribes to the required *shibboleths* of orthodoxy but knows nothing of the obedient heart that delights to do the will of the Father. That is self-deception, and Matthew returns to it again by showing how empty profession of religious intention is pilloried in the parable of the two sons. For it is not he who says 'I go, sir' and who thinks that is all that is required of him, who is approved, but he who, though he makes no promise of obedience, nevertheless does what the Father desires. Far better is performance without profession, than profession that only deceives oneself.

Again some ostensible disciples rely upon charismatic experiences, and the gifts of preaching, of exorcism, and other 'mighty works' done in the name of Christ (7:22). But their confidence too is ill-founded, Christ will say to them 'I never knew you . . .' For the gifts of the Spirit are easily counterfeited. Paul warns that though we speak the tongues of men or angels, have the gift of prophecy, understand all spiritual mysteries, and have faith enough to remove mountains, we deceive ourselves and are nothing if we have not love. Matthew recalls Jesus saying much the same, though his emphasis fell here upon obedience.

And yet other ostensible disciples rely—so Matthew appears to hint—upon their acceptance into the right religious circles, their acquaintance with the right people. This, too, is self-deception, and the remembered word of Jesus is forthright and unmistakable: taking opportunity of a chance remark of bystanders, Jesus stretched out his hand towards his disciples and said 'Here are my mother and my brothers! For whoever does the will of my Father in heaven is my brother, and sister, and mother.' To be rightly related to Christ, in simple obedience, is the only 'religious acquaintance' that counts!

It is truly remarkable in how many varied ways Matthew can make the same point, that to be a disciple of Jesus means active pursuit of right behaviour, right character, in the sight of God. For the test of all such self-deception is whether we are actually *doing the will of the Father*; while the exposure that awaits the self-deceived is (literally) 'I never knew you; depart from me, you who are working *lawlessness*'. That is to say, for Matthew righteousness implies both obedience and law, as we have next to observe.

CHAPTER SEVEN

What is *righteousness?*

The question, 'What is righteousness—What does the Lord require of us?' was a crucial issue between Matthew and his readers, whether Jewish Christians or opponents. It had been a crucial issue between Jesus and his Jewish hearers and critics also.

For the Jew, the standard of righteousness was laid down finally by divine authority and for eternity, in *Torah*, the law of God. Unfortunately, varying schools of interpretation, endless arguments about priority of this or that commandment, the slow growth of traditions 'hedging' the law about with elaborate safeguards against accidental infringement, and a very highly developed casuistry providing rules for innumerable exceptional situations, all served to make the 'final and eternal law of God' exceedingly difficult to comprehend. Six hundred and thirteen commandments, plus traditions, rules, precedents, and 'examples' quite without number, made the sacred *Torah* a bewildering exercise for the mind as well as an intolerable burden for the conscience. Earnest people, learned and simple, longed for clarification and assurance: Which is the great commandment? Which rules really matter? How can we summarise divine law and know for certain what pleases God?

To that heartfelt need, in his own time, Matthew addresses himself by presenting Jesus as God's last word on the meaning of the law.

Jesus and God's law

As background to Christ's teaching, Matthew carefully describes his attitude to the law. By innumerable small touches, he shows Jesus blameless before the law, and careful to expound the true legal position when he was accused. Joseph's legal dilemma over Mary's pregnancy is mentioned by Matthew and resolved by express divine command. When the disciples are accused of breaking the sabbath by reaping corn, Matthew adds to Mark's story Jesus' words about the legal right of the priests to place need above ritual. Healing the man with the withered hand, Jesus defends his action on the sabbath not only on moral grounds (it is always lawful to do good) as in *Mark* and *Luke*, but first cites the practice already permitted by the lawyers concerning the sabbath rescue of cattle. Similarly, in *Matthew*, Jesus meets the challenge about eating with sinners, not only with the analogy of the physician, but *first* with a quotation from the scriptures setting mercy above ritual.

Only Matthew preserves the great passage of the Sermon in which Jesus upholds and expounds the law. In chapter 23 he is shown discussing the current casuistry concerning oaths, tithes, the rules of uncleanness and 'the weightier matters of the law'. Only Matthew shows Jesus counselling the payment of the Temple tax, though claiming a 'theoretical' exemption from it; actually saying to a young man, 'If you will enter into life, keep the commandments';

or upholding the public authority of the scribes and Pharisees as sitting in Moses' seat. Matthew gives account of so few miracles (in a book so long) that we ask the reason for each one selected: that of the cleansing of a leper appears to have no particular value except that it shows Jesus scrupulously obeying the Jewish laws of hygiene and cure.

Certain of Matthew's small additions suggest the same care for the law on the part of Jesus. Jesus speaks of the instructed disciple as 'a scribe of the kingdom'; of his own teaching as his 'yoke'—the word used of *Torah*; in *Matthew* Jesus says, not that *Moses* said 'Honour your parents . . .' but that *God* commanded it. Matthew alone has the limitation of the disciples' mission spelled out to prohibit, explicitly, all contact with Gentiles and Samaritans, as strict Judaism would require. To the counsel to pray that flight, at the end of the age, should not be 'in winter' Matthew adds 'nor on the sabbath day' for strict sabbath rules prohibited more than a very limited journey.

A few slight omissions, compared with *Mark* and *Luke* point in the same direction. Jesus does not ask what Moses said about divorce: he does not need to. He does not command the forbidden Roman coin to be *brought* within the Temple. Matthew avoids the impression that Jesus threatened the Temple, or swore an oath; and he omits Mark's comment that Jesus abrogated all food laws, as well as the statement that Jesus was 'numbered with the transgressors'. Matthew does not record, as Luke does, that Jesus was once accused of eating with unwashed hands, although he does retain the reply which Jesus made (*Luke* 11:38, *Matthew* 23:25).

In the light of this desire to show Jesus careful of the law it seems curious that Matthew omits all reference to his being circumcised, until one realises that what to the Gentile Luke and his readers needed full explanation, Matthew the Jew simply takes for granted.

In a more deliberate way, too, Matthew portrays Jesus against a background of law: again and again he shows Jesus answering questions about the law, criticising the way the law was taught, confronted by the official interpreters of the law, the scribes, and by the sect most zealous for the law, the Pharisees. Well-known legal issues that rabbis had argued about for generations were brought to Jesus; he was challenged to decide between different schools of interpretation, especially between that of Shammai the Strict and that of Hillel the Gentle, leading rabbis of Christ's own earlier years.

So clearly does Matthew emphasise Jesus' concern with the law, and with the current interpretations of what is *right*, that the suggestion sometimes made, that Matthew gathered the sayings of Jesus into five great discourses to portray him as another Moses offering five new books of the law, may not be so fanciful after all. At least it is clear that to Matthew Jesus was the latest and greatest rabbi, God's own interpreter of God's own law.

The law still binding

The first pronouncement of the Master in this connection which Matthew recalls to his confused and careless church is: that the law is still binding upon the conscience of the Christian. Righteousness being still demanded, the way of righteousness, which is the revealed law of God, is still a valid obligation. The Master said:

> *'Think not that I have come to abolish the law and the prophets; I have not come to abolish them but to fulfil them. For truly I say to you, till heaven and earth pass away, not an iota, not a dot, will pass from the law until all is accomplished.'*

That is positive enough: no Pharisee could say more, or say it more plainly. But Jesus proceeds, negatively:

> *'Whoever then relaxes one of the least of these commandments and teaches men so, shall be called least in the kingdom of heaven; but he who does them and teaches them shall be called great in the kingdom of heaven.'*

Only Matthew preserves either of these sayings (5:17–19).

This unexpected insistence upon the continuity of God's law even into Christian life is carried through the Gospel with great thoroughness. The law and the prophets were *not* only 'until John'. Matthew changes that. In *Matthew*, Jesus adds to the Golden Rule (as Luke gives it) the words 'for this is the law and the prophets' as an additional motive for observing it. In the same way, to the twofold commandment of love Jesus adds—according to Matthew—the ground of its authority: 'on these two commandments depend all the law and the prophets'. Both additions imply that the law still has weight for disciples. Continuing obligation is implied too when Jesus expounds the law in detail (5:21–48);

characterises those who do not the Father's will as 'lawless'; insists that disciples respect the teaching office of the scribes 'in Moses' seat'; and blames current teaching for neglecting 'the weightier matters of the law'.

In close accord with 'not an iota, not a dot, shall pass'. Matthew four times emphasises 'all' that God requires: 'to fulfil *all* righteousness', 'until *all* is accomplished', 'observe *all* that they tell you', 'teach *all* things whatsoever I have commanded you'. That detail seems to gain significance from a parallel trait in one of the Dead Sea Scrolls, where 'all' occurs in the same way in nearly fifty passages where the willingness to drop this or that 'iota or dot' of law, as convenient, is being strongly opposed.

Matthew's summons to observe the law, like his demand for righteousness, disturbs evangelical Christians, and recalls (again) Paul's apparently opposite position. For Paul held that Christ was the end of the law; that the Christian has died to the law; that we are discharged from the law; that the law was our custodian only until Christ came (*Romans* 10:4; 7:4, 6; *Galatians* 3:23–25). Yet Paul, like Matthew, upholds the law as 'holy, and just, and good . . . We know that the law is spiritual . . .'; and he declares, as clearly as Matthew does, that 'the just requirement of the law' is still to be 'fulfilled in us' (*Romans* 7:12, 14; 8:3–4). The explanation is simple. Paul insists that by his death Christ satisfied the law's demands and 'took it out of the way', abolishing it *as a way of salvation*: men are not saved by merit gained through keeping the law; while Matthew insists that Jesus established the law, fulfilling it even in his death, and did not abolish it *as a way of life*. Thus Paul can say, 'Do we then overthrow the law by this faith? By no means! On the contrary, we uphold the law' (*Romans* 3:31)—which is precisely what Matthew is contending.

However, that the law remains binding upon Christian consciences is left in no doubt at all by the solemn and authoritative way in which Jesus interprets God's law, and lays its provisions upon all who would follow him.

What the law requires
Throughout the discussion of the law in *Matthew* it is impossible to miss the opposition between the Christian and the Judaist exposition of God's will. Jesus is shown not only charging the rabbinic authorities with not *keeping* the law through hypocrisy, but with not *understanding* the law. It is not simply a more sincere Pharisaism that is needed, but a truer insight into the divine requirements. Jesus challenges official rulings, is consulted on debatable points, warns against the teaching of the Pharisees (16:12), in each case setting his own interpretation against the prevailing view.

Thus, in the verses immediately following the saying that the law will not pass away, Jesus proceeds deliberately to set aside current statements of the law in favour of his own reading of God's will on six great issues. What 'has been said by them of old time' is stated, assessed, and corrected: as to murder, by declaring that hatred and contempt *are*

81

murder already; as to adultery, by insisting that hidden lust is equally wicked; as to divorce, by reiterating the stricter, original rule against it; as to oaths, by arguing that simple, direct truthfulness is enough, and swearing irreverent; as to retaliation, by demanding meekness and goodwill; as to love of neighbour and hatred of the enemy, by requiring 'perfect', all-inclusive love to all men, resembling the love of God. This is his new version of the law—not abolished, but reinforced, re-enacted in sharper, more searching form.

Jesus returns to oaths in chapter 15, here especially as concerned property impulsively (or angrily) vowed to the Temple—a vow that Pharisees held must be kept though it left parents without provision. Jesus condemns the substitution of human tradition for basic divine law, and likens the so-called teachers of the law to the blind leading the blind. He returns to the subject of marriage and divorce in chapter 19, here being consulted on the law's intention, and gives his own authoritative and strict interpretation so firmly that even the disciples are startled. In 12:3-7 Jesus is challenged on his understanding of the sabbath rules and Matthew greatly elaborates the reply recorded in *Mark*, by adding two further scriptural arguments; in verses 9-14 Jesus is consulted about the sabbath rules on healing, and again his reply is lengthened in *Matthew* by an appeal to what the authorities themselves allow when property rather than people is involved. Matthew clearly thinks of Jesus as teacher of righteousness and interpreter of the law without peer.

But how did Jesus' understanding of God's law

differ from that of the rabbis? By what principles, different from the accepted rules, did Jesus expound the will of God? The answer is threefold:

(i) Jesus certainly made the law's demands more radical and searching, by pressing beyond the forbidden *act*, as of murder or adultery, to the state of mind and heart behind the act, as hatred, contempt, or lust. Similarly, Jesus caricatured sharply the external forms of piety, such as almsgiving, public prayer, fasting, which though ostentatiously 'religious' lacked all the sincerity which might make the outward act acceptable with God. Though Jesus nowhere praises the cultivation of personal character that neglects the out-going deed of kindness, mercy and generosity, neither does he commend the external deed, done 'to be seen of men', without the compassion, humility, and love, which alone give men's acts their moral value.

The effect of this 'interior' view is far-reaching. Law can take no account of inward states; it is the weakness of all legalism in religion that it must be external in its judgements, assessing only the visible, measurable deed. Hence, by radicalising, internalising the law's requirements, Jesus was already undermining legalism altogether as a category of religious life. This was immediately evident. For though pressing the law inwards upon the heart sharply raised its demands, as to murder, adultery, swearing, it actually set the written law aside as to divorce (in 19:3–9), and as to retaliation and the attitude to enemies. The required standard here, as with Paul's 'fruit of the Spirit', was something no *law* could prescribe.

(ii) Jesus certainly, too, in some cases, pressed behind the written enactment of the law to the original divine intention which the law imperfectly expressed. Thus in 19:1–12, on marriage and divorce, Jesus' reinterpretation of the rules proceeds, first, by passing beyond the permissive legislation to the hardness of men's hearts, which alone justified divorce as a protection for the rejected wife; then, secondly, Jesus appealed to the original will of the Creator in instituting marriage. Moses may have conceded, '*but from the beginning it was not so . . .*'

In essence, this is not merely an appeal to antiquity, to which rule was the older; but to the character of God—which rule better expressed the divine mind. That appeal, in effect a deliberate assessment of the moral value of particular laws in the light of what is known of God, is urged in the same way against the popular slogan, 'you shall love your neighbour and hate your enemy'. To be sons of the Father, Jesus replies, we must be like the Father—whatever the rules say: and he 'makes his sun rise on the evil and on the good, and sends rain on the just and the unjust'. The same principle is applied to the sabbath laws: Jesus appeals to Hosea's dictum about God, 'I desire mercy and not sacrifice'; and he challenges the comparison in *value* which (according to the lawyers) God places upon a sheep and upon a man.

There can be no question of the far-reaching consequences of this insight, too. Much in the Mosaic law offends the modern Christian conscience: trial by poisoned cup, animal sacrifice, circumcision as a badge of religious privilege, food-tabus, the notion of corporate guilt as there understood. This is because in the gospel we have learned more clearly the character of God. With Christ's own authority, we assess, select, and reinterpret the ancient rules in the light of all Christ has shown us of God's mind and love. The scribes and Pharisees were not mistaken when they saw in this whole approach a serious danger to their own position as interpreters of an absolute, unalterable code.

This is the answer to the question, which Matthew's Gospel must provoke: *How much* of the ancient law did Matthew hold to be binding upon the Christian conscience? Must we take 'not an iota, not a dot' quite literally? The answer must be, 'The law is binding, but *Christ* will tell you what the law is'. One limiting principle is the known character of God (the other remains to be mentioned). Matthew himself does not appear to question the ceremonial laws (sacrifice 5:23-24; temple-taxation 17:24, 25; the Sabbath 24:20; fasting 6:16, 17; tithing 23:23) though these do not express the 'exceeding righteousness' required of disciples. Paul, too, upheld such pious laws *for himself and other Jews* (Acts 20:16; 21:18-26). The other examples discussed by Matthew: adultery, divorce, murder, truth-telling, retaliation, attitude to enemies, suggest that his insistence that the law remains binding has in view almost entirely the *moral* demands of the law, as 'moral' is interpreted by the character of God, revealed in Christ.

(iii) As a particular instance of his appeal to the character of God, yet one which in the end totally superseded the ancient interpretation of the law, Jesus subordinated every law to *love*. This is implied, in detail, in what Jesus says of the law's demands concerning divorce, sabbath healings, sacrifice, tithing: motives and attitudes to others are the supreme considerations. But it becomes explicit, and determinative, when Jesus is consulted on the much canvassed question, 'Which is the great commandment in the law?'

The question involves the issue of priority, '*Which is the most important commandment*? and the possibility of epitomising the many commandments into one comprehensive, memorable rule.

The rabbis themselves asked 'What is the smallest portion of scripture on which all the regulations of the Torah hang?' One suggested reply was, 'In all your ways remember him'. But the usual reply, in Rabbinic summaries and comparisons of 'hard' and 'easy' commandments, was that each commandment is as important as the rest. 'Behave towards an easy commandment exactly as towards a difficult one, for you do not know what reward will be given for the commandments'. 'The scriptures make the easiest among the easy commandments equal to the hardest among the hard'. 'Woe to us, that the scripture attaches the same weight to the easy as to the hard'. In practice, of course, poorer and busier people had to assume some scale of priorities among the innumerable rules of godliness presented to them by wealthy and more leisured lawyers.

So when a lawyer publicly asks Jesus the popular question, which of the six hundred and thirteen commandments could be held to be so essential as to embrace the rest, Jesus answered, not with some revolutionary 'Christian' principle, but with an ancient Levitical commandment: 'You shall love the Lord your God with all your heart, and with all your soul, and with all your mind. This is the great and first commandment. And a second is like it, You shall love your neighbour as yourself'. So far Matthew follows Mark's account, except that Mark records Jesus adding, 'There is no other commandment greater than these', and the lawyer heartily agrees, with the comment that such love 'is more than all whole burnt offerings and sacrifices'.

In *Mark*, therefore, the priority of the love commandment, even over the Temple ritual, is the sole issue, and Matthew does not desert that: 'This is the great and first commandment'. But Matthew adds that Jesus said, 'On these two commandments depend all the law and the prophets'. The addition declares plainly the further point, that the twofold love-commandment contains within itself the norm and essence of all commandments: so that if this is fulfilled, all the rest likewise are accomplished.

Paul, too, so understood Jesus: 'He who loves his neighbour has fulfilled the law . . . any other commandment . . . summed up in this sentence, "You shall love your neighbour as yourself." . . . Love is the fulfilling of the law' (*Romans* 13:8–10).

That pronouncement is revolutionary. Here legalism gives place to love, Judaism to Christianity, Moses to Jesus. For what Matthew shows Jesus doing is making love *sufficient* as the summary of all God's requirements, not only as more important than anything else, but as *including* everything else. In the performance of this duty, all other duties are performed. The formal equality of all commandments, in importance and obligation, is abandoned; the love-commandment is raised to become the canon for the interpretation of the whole *Torah*, the sufficient law. Sacrifice, tithe, divorce, sabbath, on all issues the only question that is important, Jesus will say, is 'What does love to God and my neighbour dictate?' In the end, all *can* be summarised in one neat and memorable precept; for the meaning of love, the only necessary comment is the Golden Rule: 'Whatever you wish that men would do to you, do so to them; for this is the law and the prophets' (7:12).

So, within the forms and terms of legalism, Jesus destroyed all legalism!

The Prince of rabbis
By these three principles of interpretation, Jesus (as Matthew portrays him) transforms the whole law while insisting that God's claim upon man's obedience remains absolute, and complete. Jesus is shown as the Interpreter Extraordinary of the divine requirements, the Definer of what righteousness means; if not a new Moses, then the Prince of rabbis, the final authority on the will of God and on the standards by which human behaviour will be judged.

What this stupendous claim meant to Matthew's Christian readers, distressed by the break with Judaism, we can measure from the wide popularity and power his book came to possess in the church. Its effect on those still hesitating, as they were urged not to disobey the sacred law in rebellion, but to hear it reinterpreted in freedom, we can only guess. But what this strong insistence upon the validity, and the meaning, of God's law *for Christians* meant to a church confused and careless about ethical questions, we may judge from its impact upon our own hearts. In days of amoral permissiveness, both outside and even within the church of Christ, Matthew's Gospel still speaks with immense force and relevance. For it conducts us straight back, as Matthew intended it should, to the feet of the Master himself, Lord of conscience, the very incarnation of the holy and loving will of God.

Jesus is the Christian lawgiver; disciples must be taught to observe whatever he has commanded. But his yoke is easy, his burden is light, bringing rest and refreshment to the heart, because Jesus establishes God's law, not by fear nor by the self-righteous hope of merit, but inwardly, within the heart that loves God. And by his revelation of God as kingly Father and fatherly King, Redeemer of sinful men and Friend of all, he *wins* the love that the law commands. John was to say, later, 'His commandments are not burdensome'. Matthew, too, had discovered that the judgements of the Lord are true and righteous altogether, more to be desired than gold, sweeter also than honey. For had not Jesus said,

Come to me, all who labour and are heavy-laden, and I will give you rest. Take my yoke upon you, and learn from me; for I am gentle and lowly in heart, and you will find rest for your souls. For my yoke is easy, and my burden is light.

CHAPTER EIGHT

The Church and the future: judgement

A clear demand for righteousness, and the presentation of Jesus as the lawgiver for the church, do not quite satisfy Matthew's concern about the condition of the church. He is eager also to lift the church's eyes to the future, that she might see her present life in the light of the final purposes of God. But the first future reality that Matthew beholds is *judgement*.

The certainty of judgement

For *Matthew* is not only the Gospel of righteousness, of the church, of the teaching, and of the law: it is no less plainly the Gospel of judgement. That word occurs twelve times; 'day of judgement' four times; the idea of reward ten times; and phrases like 'outer darkness', 'weeping', 'gnashing of teeth', a further nine times. Nearly all the great pictures, texts, and warnings about Judgement Day were rescued from the fading tradition of what Jesus had said by Matthew, and thrust upon the attention of a church which, as he felt, sadly needed to recall them. These include the parables of the Sheep and Goats, of the bridesmaids shut out of Messiah's wedding feast, of the ill-clad guest ejected from the banquet, of the sorting out of the wheat from the weeds, and of the good fish from the bad—all this we owe entirely to Matthew's diligence in adding to *Mark*.

It is significant of Matthew's purpose that in the parable of the wheat and the weeds the main theme is the need for patience; but the explanation of the parable, now annexed to it, concentrates on the certainty of the divine destruction: patience is not mentioned. The church *will* get sorted out: church-membership offers no security. Matthew preserved, too, Christ's words about judgement in hell for those who treat a brother with contempt; the warning that in the end even our words will be judged; the testimony against us that will be given by unexpected witnesses like the people of Nineveh and the Queen of Sheba, if we obey not the gospel.

Curiously, Matthew has at least six passages, or ideas, which he has recorded twice:

the hand or eye causing to sin, 5:29, 30 equals 18:8–9

good or bad trees, 7:17–20 very like 12:33

Sodom's example, 10:15 equals 11:24

'Watch!' 24:42 equals 25:13

Messiah cutting down trees, 3:10 equals 7:19

The first will be last, 19:30 equals 20:16

and each of them mentions, in some fashion, the last divine assessment: hell, burning by fire, day of judgement, day of the Lord's coming, the reversal of human judgement. This is a good example of Matthew's reiteration for emphasis and solemnity.

Moreover, Matthew constructs his fifth great discourse wholly from sayings of Jesus about the future, full of foreboding of divine verdicts, and calling upon disciples to *watch* at all times. All this, too, is *Matthew* only.

Plainly, for Matthew, God is the King who settles accounts. This is said three times, and there is a shudder in the phrase: he settles accounts with his debtors; we shall give account of what we say; and we shall give account of the stewardship of our talents. The call to take up the cross brings with it warning that the Son of man comes to repay every man for what he has done about it. Mark shares with Matthew the parable of the vineyard, ending with the prophecy that the sacred soil will be taken from Israel and given to others; by the time Matthew wrote, Jerusalem had fallen, but Matthew's version still closes with a warning relevant to his own readers: 'Therefore I tell you, *the kingdom of God* will be taken from you and given to a nation producing the fruits of it'. What was spoken by Jesus to unbelieving Jews as they prepared to reject Jesus as Messiah, is applied by Matthew to all who fail to yield fruit for God. Plainly, in the traditions which he alone preserves, Matthew is faithfully preserving the warning of the 'sign of the Son of Man in heaven, when all the earth shall mourn'.

Added to all this are the further references to judgement which Matthew shares with Luke. The approaching storm, which shall test the foundations of every man's house; the coming day when Jesus shall say to some 'I never knew you'; those banished to gnash their teeth in isolation and darkness; the illustration of Sodom's fate (Matthew adds Gomorrah for good measure); the healthy fear of him who can cast souls into hell; the warnings to Chorazin,

Bethsaida and Capernaum, which are much more fully recorded in *Matthew*; the setting of the disciples' mission in the light of the approaching harvest-time; a warning that Noah's days and circumstances will be repeated; and the astonishing figure of the divine burglar, the thief in the night: all this adds yet further weight to Matthew's own contribution to the record of what Jesus said about judgement.

So much cannot be ignored, or explained away as merely eloquent metaphor underlining the seriousness of moral decisions: it is the final message Matthew has to give to the careless and confused conscience of the church he knew. There is no substitute for righteousness now, and no shelter from judgement hereafter. God will surely and fairly settle accounts. So persistent an emphasis suggests that Matthew believed that the fear of judgement had faded from the conscience of his church, as we know it has from the conscience of the modern church. Indeed, the future dimension has largely disappeared from Christian thought and faith. The picture of the great white throne no longer frightens anyone, as the notion of a stern God of right and justice, one of too pure eyes to look upon evil, no longer nerves Christian resistance to temptation or stiffens conviction into martyrdom. In an age of grey compromise and expediency, the *doctrine* of judgement has ceased to be a *motive*: Matthew met that situation with words of Jesus himself.

Who are the arraigned?
We miss Matthew's urgent warning if we imagine that divine judgement is only for the sinner. Again

93

and again Matthew insists it will fall upon the church. Wheat and weeds are in God's field, which is the *kingdom*; good and bad fish are in the kingdom net. The mitigating pleas which will be made in that day, and which Matthew shows will be rejected: inherited privileges, profession of Jesus as 'Lord, Lord', close relationship with Jesus, hearing or knowing the sayings of Jesus, possession of charismatic powers, of prophecy, exorcism, and miracle are all pleas which *Christians*, or apparent Christians, would make.

The call to self-discipline, with the alternative of eternal fire (in chapter 18) is set within the discussion of Christian relationships, as the whole passage on suffering, and treatment of the immature and erring, places Christian behaviour in the light of ultimate divine judgement. In the parable of the wedding feast as now recorded (possibly framed from fragments of two original parables), the good and evil are together at the feast by royal invitation. The final truth about membership in the church is still to be revealed: 'many are called, but few are chosen'; 'he that endures to the end shall be saved'.

The 'Woes' pronounced upon the characteristic vices of the Pharisees would have as little relevance for Matthew's readers as for ourselves were it not implied that such vices arise also within the church. The opening verses of this passage (23:1–12) are expressly addressed to the Christian congregation; and throughout, some eleven times, the horizon and viewpoint are the end-time of divine judgement. Similarly, the discourse on the future is for 'disciples' (24:1, 3, 9; 25:13) and foreshadows judgement on the wicked *servants* of the Lord, on bridesmaids at his wedding, on the bearers of talents he bestowed, and the sheep and goats within his flock, though, in this final picture, no distinction is made between Jew and Christian, believers and un-believers, except by the verdict of the Judge.

Dealing with penitents unable to believe in the freeness and fullness of divine forgiveness through faith in Christ alone, Paul gave assurance that there is no condemnation for those who are in Christ Jesus; given penitence and faith, no divine rejection need be feared. Faced with nominal church members, of uncertain loyalty and careless conscience, Matthew asserts that divine judgement *will* sift the church in the end. Yet here again, on this wider view of the needed truth, Paul agrees with Matthew: 'He will render to every man according to his works: to those who by patience in well-doing seek for glory and honour and immortality, he will give eternal life; but for those who are factious and do not obey the truth, but obey wickedness, there will be wrath and fury . . . God shows no partiality . . . We must all appear before the judgement seat of Christ, so that each one may receive good or evil, according to what he has done in the body' (*Romans* 2:6–11; *2 Corinthians* 5:10). John, too, records a saying of Jesus which suggests that no divine judgement need be feared: 'Truly, truly I say to you, he who hears my word and believes him who sent me has eternal life; *he does not come into judgement*, but has passed from death to life'. Given the con-ditions named, acceptance and life are already

assured. This accords with John's whole presentation of 'the last things' as already in train.
For John, as for Paul and for Matthew, divine
judgement is a real event: 'the Father has given
all judgement to the Son . . . has given him
authority to execute judgement also'. But the
judgement is *contemporary* ('For judgement I
came into this world . . . now is the judgement
of this world'); it occurs as men react to Jesus
('this is the judgement, that light has come . . .
and men loved darkness rather than light'); and it
continues through the work of the Spirit ('he will
convince the world of sin . . . of judgement').
Nevertheless, for John the time will come when
this contemporary and continuing judgement
will (so to speak) be made overt and 'public' and
final: 'Do not marvel at this, for the hour is coming
when all who are in the tombs will hear his voice
and come forth, those who have done good, to the
resurrection of life, and those who have done evil,
to the resurrection of judgement' (*John* 3:19;
5:22–29; 9:39; 12:31; 16:8, 11).

Thus both Paul and John insist that those who
truly believe have nothing to fear at the end;
Matthew is warning that some within the very
mixed church have everything to fear, for *all* will
be 'sorted out'. It is of this final revelation of the
true state and ultimate destiny of every man, that
Matthew makes so much.

Matthew, at any rate, is very clear that Christians
generally may not presume upon divine acceptance,
nor upon escaping from divine judgement. As we
saw, it is possible to see in so many of Matthew's

characters illustrations of over-confident self-deception, and we might add to those already suggested the foolish man who, knowing the counsel of Christ, yet builds unwisely; the weeds which masquerade as wheat; the bad trees which appear as sound; the ill-prepared bridesmaids—all these are self-deceived about their status and security in Christ. The same sayings which (as their position shows) Matthew intends as barbs to deflate presumption, 'Many that are first shall be last' and 'Many are called but few are chosen', are also premonitions of final and most solemn judgement upon Christian profession.

The verdict

Two aspects of the nature of divine judgement, as Matthew foresaw it, demand attention. One is that judgement will be upon works, upon things done or not done, and not upon profession or belief. This is most clear in the parable of the Sheep and Goats, where no distinction at all between people is mentioned, except as some have kept the essential, summarising law of love—fed the hungry, clothed the naked, visited the sick and imprisoned, and some have not. That is all that matters in the end; that is the only 'righteousness' according to divine law as Jesus interpreted it, and that is final. The law which Jesus came to establish, to interpret and to impose, is the law by which men are judged at last.

Some seek to evade this conclusion by devious interpretations of the parable, but that the divine judgement falls upon works does not by any means rest on that passage alone. Throughout *Matthew*, the criterion of judgement is simply who does, and who does not do, 'the will of the Father in heaven'. In chapter 12, doing the Father's will decides who is brother and sister to Christ. In 7:21 doing the will of the Father decides who shall enter the kingdom: it is by this standard that mere knowledge, profession, charismatic experiences, are set aside— they are no substitute for obedience. In 21:28–32 the only issue between sons who say 'Yes' and sons who say 'No' is, 'Which eventually did the will of the Father?' Judgement by that divine will covers our words, of which we shall give account; the way we have actually built the house of life; the fruits of living, by which the sound or diseased condition of our nature will be revealed; 'what every man has done', for which the Son of man will repay each in time; and the garments of character in which we present ourselves in the King's presence. Words, deeds, habits, character, the outcome of life: on these the final judgement rests. God judges by facts and deeds; the standard is the will of the Father; and Christ interpreted that will as love.

Here once more it is right to observe that both Paul and John agree with Matthew, that the basis of the final judgement will be works, deeds, character (*Romans* 2:6–11; *2 Corinthians* 5:10; *John* 5:29).

But if such is the basis, the verdict is equally unexpected, for it includes (at least) the decision as to who shall eventually find a place in the kingdom of God. There is little doubt that Matthew equates this with entering into *life*.

Compare 7:14 with 7:21; 19:17 with 19:23; and 5:20 with 5:29, 30 ('avoiding hell') equals 18:8, 9 ('entering life').

In *Mark*, in *Luke*, and in some passages in *Matthew*, the kingdom is established already; it is 'at hand' in Christ's lifetime, immediately available for all who will enter by becoming as a child, surrendering to the King's reign. Matthew says that this was the initial proclamation of Jesus; of some Jesus says without hesitation 'theirs is the kingdom', as of others it could be said, 'the kingdom of heaven has come upon you'. Matthew is well aware that the inauguration of the long-foretold kingdom has begun.

Yet the final decision concerning membership of that kingdom is still future, because the ultimate establishment of the kingdom is yet to come. Disciples do not yet know who is in the kingdom and who is not: that is why the Son of man will sit upon the throne of his glory and apportion to men their places, saying to some 'Come, ye blessed of my Father, inherit the kingdom prepared for you . . .'. *Inherit*—for it is not yet yours; *prepared*—for the position is only now being finalised. So too Christians must pray till the end of time, 'Thy kingdom come . . .' and all their days '*Seek* first the kingdom . . .'. Many 'will come' in the future to sit in Messiah's kingdom; and Jesus will drink wine one day with the disciples in the Father's kingdom—but not yet.

Again, we must wait until the Son of man comes before we shall see the kingdom purged of all 'causes of offence and all evil-doers'; then, but not till then, will the righteous shine in the kingdom. Even in that day not all who say 'Lord, Lord . . .' shall *enter* the kingdom—a point still to be decided. Indeed, and ominously, the kingdom may be taken away even from those who already 'have' it: 'I tell you, the kingdom of God will be taken away from you and given to a nation producing the fruits of it' (21:42).

A surprising verse: but we must not rewrite it to mean 'taken from the Jews who ought to have inherited it and did not . . .'. That is not what Jesus said; besides, how can you 'take away' what they never had? It is possible that the words refer to the *opportunity* of the kingdom rather than to its *possession*, though that again is not what Jesus said, and would have little relevance for Matthew's readers. Perhaps 'kingdom' here is equivalent to life under the Old Testament theocracy.

Matthew's overall view of the kingdom of God seems to rest upon the vision of Daniel, of the great world powers coming one by one in the fashion of beasts to the Ancient of Days to receive their dominion; followed by one not like a beast but in form human, like 'a son of man', who came on clouds to receive a *humane* kingdom: 'And to him was given dominion and glory and kingdom, that all peoples, nations, and languages should serve him; his dominion is an everlasting dominion, which shall not pass away, and his kingdom one that shall not be destroyed'. This surely is the source of Matthew's picture of the Son of man coming on the clouds with the holy angels to sit upon the throne of his glory—

but not yet, not while Jesus still walks the earth. The point at which the Son of man received the kingdom is (for Matthew) between resurrection and ascension: for then at last, his humiliation, meekness and submission over, he can say, 'All power is given unto me in heaven and on earth'.

Then Jesus came into his glory. But meanwhile, as Matthew insists, the kingdom has weeds within it, causes of evil, and none yet knows who is and who is not within the kingdom. It is all 'prepared' but who shall eventually inherit? Only the angels can separate false from true: the verdict is God's.

That is why Matthew's warnings are addressed almost exclusively to disciples. He is concerned lest the misunderstanding about free grace, needing no merit to obtain forgiveness, lull the church into entirely false complacency, a perilous imagined security, which misses the kingdom in the end. Servants may prove faithless; those sitting at the Table may betray; bridesmaids may be shut out; some who think the kingdom belongs to them may find it taken from them; and—most startling of all—one may have been forgiven, *but God can take forgiveness back* (18:32–35): for so did the lord of the unforgiving servant, in the parable, and Jesus adds 'So also my heavenly Father will do to every one of you . . .'.

Even the solemn reminders that without righteousness we shall *never enter* the kingdom; that being weeds within the kingdom we may yet be *purged from it*; that thinking we possess the kingdom we may find it taken from us, are not more stern than that dreadful warning—that the unforgiving shall find themselves after all unforgiven.

What can we do?

But Matthew has no intention of merely frightening Christians, even though a false security is the sort of peril it is well to be saved from by any means at hand. Matthew has positive purpose in thus thrusting upon the church the solemn words of her Master about judgement: he believed that the final sorting-out can be anticipated, here and now, if we are in earnest, and are prepared to draw sharp lines, to reaffirm loyalties, to redefine commitment.

For sifting, separation, is another of the ethical themes in this rich and practical Gospel: not the separation of the church from the world (that is not mentioned in *Matthew*) but the separation of wheat from weeds, good fish from bad, those who use talents from those who neglect them, foolish brides-maids from wise, those who remain at the King's banquet from the one 'thrust outside', one woman from beside another in the field, one man from another at the mill. Such sorting out of people goes on all through Matthew's Gospel. *We* are warned not to attempt it: 'judge not, that you be not judged—for whatever measure you use to assess others will be used to assess you'. It is angels' work: God must do it—and he will.

But *for ourselves* it would be well to do some sorting out at once. Though the Christian community may be mixed, *we must not be*. One whole passage of the mountain Sermon underlines the need for self-assessment, for inward sifting, while we have time. We cannot lay up treasures both on earth and in heaven, we have only one heart, which cannot be in two places. We cannot serve two masters: it is God or mammon. We cannot enter by the narrow gate and by the wide, nor walk the broad path and the restricted, lonely road to life, both at the same time. We are either sheep or wolves, sound trees or diseased, bearing good fruit or bitter. We build on Christ's foundation—on his instructions—or we build on sand in our own folly. Eight times the relentless either-or: that cannot be accidental. We must not judge others, but we had better judge ourselves, while still we may. We must let truth and the rigid test of *doing the Father's will* sort us out now: or divine judgement will do it when amendment is no longer possible.

It is just possible that one obscure paragraph of the same Sermon means precisely that. We cannot be sure: Luke places it elsewhere, and Matthew links it with the charge to seek reconciliation with an offended brother. As we read it there, it seems but prudent advice to compromise:

> 'Make friends quickly with your accuser, while you are going with him to court, lest your accuser hand you over to the judge, and the judge to the guard, and you be put in prison; truly, I say to you, you will never get out till you have paid the last penny' (5:25–26).

Of course it may be that Jesus meant exactly that: better to compromise than to drive issues implacably to extremes. Yet should one compromise with an *accuser* if one is innocent, or if one is guilty? Are we to avoid the trial of impartial justice, or the penalty we deserve? And what has compromise with an accuser to do with reconciling a brother? It is not easy to be sure what Jesus intended here.

But as Jesus spoke the words, and with the passage on sorting out our own position clearly in mind, it *may be* that the Master was referring not to human courts and accusers but to God's judgement-seat and the accusations we there face. Was Jesus urging that we constantly *anticipate* the judgement we shall ultimately face, and put things right with God *now*, with meek and penitent heart, while there is still time?

That is, at any rate, what Matthew says, quite clearly, to his church, in this Gospel of the last judgement.

CHAPTER NINE

The Church and the future: hope

Loss of the future dimension of the Christian faith affects not only the expectation of judgement but the hope of ultimate victory, of the coming of the kingdom and the advent of Christ. Modern Christians scarcely know what to think about the future: the 'coming on the clouds' is as obscure an idea as 'the great white throne', and Christianity is the poorer for lack of advent-excitement.

Of course, we profess beliefs about 'the last things' and hold opinions, sometimes strongly, about the fulfilment of prophecy. In some circles, futurist programmes are an accepted pledge of orthodoxy. But do we *live* by hope, or by fear? We insure our homes, keep up our pension-payments, count upon tomorrow, organise for distant retirement, like any pagan who has no expectation that the future will differ from the past. Like him, too, we have no thought that the future is other than in our own hands to prepare. The living anticipation of an end is no urgent motive-force in most modern discipleship. Matthew seems to have felt that the same was true of the church he knew.

'Hope deferred . . .'
For even yet, over fifty years after the resurrection,

nearly twenty-five years after the cataclysmic destruction of Jerusalem, the church still asked, 'Where is the promise of his coming?' What is even worse, some have ceased to ask. This is clear from Matthew's way of underlining hope.

Matthew adds to *Mark*, as something which Mark omitted but which the church urgently needs to hear, the parable of the Talents—essentially a lesson on *what to do while the Lord is away*. In it one sees the church, in the three groups described: the gifted and hard-working; the less gifted but equally zealous, who also are commended; and those who do nothing. But it is upon the last group that Matthew's emphasis falls, as he remembers the story. About these arises a heated discussion, and sharp words: for these are the people for whom the years of delay are wasted years, who blame the absent Lord for harsh terms and do nothing for him. It is thus clearly a parable of the interim-period, with lessons on advent-expectation. Luke has it too, though he speaks of a different currency and the distribution is differently arranged; but Matthew adds a significant phrase which Luke lacks, 'Now *after a long time* the master of those servants came and settled accounts . . .'. That signals Matthew's sense of what the church is feeling: '. . . a long time'.

This must be intentional, for it recurs, even more plainly, in the account of the wicked servant who misuses the interim-period before the coming of his lord to get drunk and ill-treat the other servants. The explanation is explicit: 'that wicked servant says to himself, "My master is delayed . . .".' That is what Matthew's church was muttering: the Master delays his coming!

Even more clearly, in another parable which only Matthew preserves, the problems occasioned by the delay are the whole point. A marriage is on foot, and the bridesmaids await the coming of the bridegroom. Five are prudent, reliable girls, but five are foolish, improvident, unready. Why? *Not* because they slept, all did that; but because they did not *provide for a delay*. The *foolish* ones are the eager second-adventists who counted on an immediate return of Christ and did not lay in store sufficient oil to last the long night through. The wise attendant on the Lord is ready whenever he chooses to come, soon or late; the foolish are those who, excited at first, cannot cope with delay. Matthew's preservation and use of such a story eloquently reveals his concern about the deferred hope that robbed some fellow-members of their zeal.

All that Matthew has said about the judgement illustrates his interest in the last things, as does also his fifth great 'discourse'. In the latter, a curious *motif* of delay is inter-woven with the certainty of hope. The disciples say 'Lord, tell us when . . .' and that question, current in Matthew's church, sets the theme. The essence of Christ's answer (if we read the discourse carefully) is 'The end is not yet'.

'Take heed that no one leads you astray . . . you will hear of wars and rumours of wars; see that you are not alarmed; for this must take place, but the end is not yet. For nation will rise against nation . . . famine . . . earthquakes . . . all this is but the beginning. . . . Tribulation . . . hated . . . many fall away . . . false prophets. . . . But he who endures to the end will be saved. And this gospel of the kingdom will be preached throughout the whole world . . . then the end will come . . .'.

There follow further details of a considerable programme of preparatory events: the desolating sacrilege in the holy place, flight, and great tribulation, false Christs, great messianic excitement, and *after* all this, 'the sign of the Son of man in heaven'. 'But of that day and hour no one knows'.

All these are notes not of adventist excitement but of deliberate delay. There is certainty, and even urgency in some words: 'Truly I say, this generation will not pass till all things take place . . . When you see all these things, you know that he is near, at the very gates'. But when the church asks, 'Well, why has it not happened?' Matthew recalls Christ's words, 'the end is not yet . . . This is but the beginning'. Matthew's problem is that deferred hope has destroyed expectancy: he would explain the delay as just what Jesus warned would happen, and quicken the certainty that nevertheless the Lord *will* come.

The problem of the delayed advent troubled other New Testament writers. Paul once thought the coming of Christ so near that difficulties over mixed marriages and over slavery need not concern Christians—'the time has grown very short'. Yet he rebukes (in much the same way as the parable of the Bridesmaids does) those so excited about Christ's 'imminent return' as to be unprepared for diligent and sensible use of the 'meantime' (*2 Thessalonians* 2:1–8: note the interweaving of certainty and delay; and 3:6–13). The phrase, 'Where is the promise of his coming?' is from *2 Peter*, and the reply there made is that there is no 'soon' or 'late' with God: a thousand years in God's sight are as one day. Besides, the delay is merciful, that all might be ready.

John's Gospel, too, wrestles with the problem of the delayed advent, emphasising that while a 'coming' has still to be fulfilled, the coming of Christ in the Spirit was an immediate and glorious fact, already fulfilled. The answer of Luke, like that of Matthew, is to recall in the light of the delay the things which Jesus had said must happen first; and so to begin to 'programme' the last things, showing that excitement about an 'imminent, any-moment return' was not justified. We must live soberly meanwhile, but the Lord *will* come!

'. . . *Makes the heart sick*'
Matthew's concern is ever practical, rather than theoretical or theological. The mood of deferred hope, of disappointment, the feeling that the future is empty, can have serious consequences among church members, not least among those committed to the service of Christ as leaders and activists. Members grow restive, are easily attracted to new excitements, new cults, prophetic schemes, and promises of imminent victory and success, or to marvellous new spiritual experiences which some novel version of the gospel offers to bestow. A church without hope grows bored; and spiritual boredom generates heresies, deviationist sects, off-beat cults, and diversionary spiritual excitements.

Seeing it all, Matthew reminded the church of the Master's explicit warnings of these dangers, warnings repeated four times for those wistfully longing for the Christ, or despairing of his coming.

'Take heed that no one leads you astray. For many will come in my name, saying, "I am the Christ", and they will lead many astray . . . And many false prophets will arise and lead many astray . . . For false Christs and false prophets will arise and show great signs and wonders, so as to lead astray, if possible, even the elect.'

That is one common consequence of disappointment and delayed fulfilment: there are always some people in the church ready to exploit it by offering some ingenious spiritual 'gimmick' that satisfies for a season.

Alarm at the state of the world is a second symptom of future-deprivation. 'You will hear of wars and rumours of wars; see that you are not alarmed. . . . For nation will rise against nation, and kingdom against kingdom, and there will be famines and earthquakes in various places. . . . Then they will deliver you up to tribulation, and put you to death; and you will be hated by all nations for my name's sake. . . . For then there will be great tribulation such as has not been from the beginning of the world until now. . . . And if those days had not been shortened, no human being would be saved . . .'.

'See that you are not alarmed . . .'—but if we have no advent hope to cling to, what does the future hold but strife and decadence, increasing persecution, the ultimate defeat of spiritual values? Apostolic

Christians had always greeted the unseen with a cheer, being insured against future-shock by their adventist certainties; by Matthew's time, such insurance was devalued, the certainties were shaken, and the future frightened them, as it frightens us.

For a third symptom of faded hope, 'many will fall away, and betray one another, and hate one another . . . And because wickedness is multiplied, most men's love will grow cold'. All that Matthew has said of the mixed quality of the church, of the blunted Christian conscience and the dwindling of zeal (as in the parable of the Talents) is directly related to the lost expectation of Christ's coming:

'Blessed is that servant whom his master when he comes' will find faithful. 'But if that wicked servant says to himself, "My master is delayed" and begins to beat his fellow-servants, and eats and drinks with the drunken, the master of that servant will come. . . .'

Plainly, deferred hope has more serious spiritual consequences than the danger of being led astray, or becoming alarmed about the future.

The truth is that a church without a forward-dimension to her faith will find that much else gets out of true perspective. No Christian, and no fellowship of Christians, can live joyfully and fruitfully upon the past only, nor even on past and present together. Without keen and well-founded anticipation, eagerness dies away, initiative for change loses its mainspring, resilience in adversity dwindles to mere doggedness, faith becomes querulous, and the price of loyalty begins to seem too high. Spiritual health requires the constant tonic stimulus of hope.

Matthew's cure

Faced with this pastoral need, Matthew is not content to warn and to exhort. Above all he desires to face the church again with the figure of the Master. To do this convincingly. it was necessary to recall different aspects in the revelation of Christ to men; for as the story unfolds, both majesty and meekness are revealed in him who was both Servant and Messiah.

On the one hand are the authority of word and deed which marks Matthew's portrait of Jesus; the regal calm of his bearing among the crowds and before his enemies; the constant reminder of his messianic lineage and claim; the way every detail of his story had been foretold; scenes like his supernatural birth, the visit of the magi, his baptism and transfiguration, and the entry to Jerusalem. Jesus is God's elect, divinely anointed to inaugurate God's kingdom; he bears all the great titles of the expected mighty one: Immanuel, Son of David, Son of man, Son of God, Servant of the Lord, and 'Lord' itself (which Matthew uses constantly where Mark says 'teacher'). In drawing attention to such majesty, Matthew plays down the contrary suggestion, such as that only God can forgive, the denial that Jesus is 'good', the questions he asked, some of the criticisms uttered against him. loose references to his emotions, or to his 'inability' to work miracles (e.g. at Nazareth).

Despite all this, Matthew does not hide but rather delights in the lowliness and humiliation of

Jesus, as one always utterly obedient to the will of the Father, content to submit to what is 'fitting' to fulfil all righteousness, even to taking our infirmities and bearing our *diseases* (8:17). He is the lowly king whom Zechariah foresaw, 'humble and mounted on an ass' and surrounded by children. He invites men to take upon themselves the yoke of his law just because he is gentle, and lowly in heart; and for the same reason he can set a child amid the disciples not only as the example of humility but as the meaning of greatness. His counsel for them is but his maxim for himself: 'Whoever exalts himself will be humbled, and whoever humbles himself will be exalted'.

So Jesus is 'spoken against', his words are 'not kept'; men call even the Master of the house 'Beelzebul'. He is rebuked by Peter, betrayed by Judas, delivered by Jews 'to the Gentiles to be mocked, and scourged, and crucified'. And when Jesus withdraws from the first threats of his enemies to destroy him, Matthew draws deliberate attention, to this self-imposed humiliation with words of Isaiah,

'Behold, my servant whom I have chosen . . .
He will not wrangle or cry aloud,
  nor will anyone hear his voice in the streets;
he will not break a bruised reed
  or quench a smouldering wick. . . .'

It may be that the contrast between these two features of Matthew's portrait underlies the curious question about the Son of David being nevertheless David's Lord: at any rate, the two features are there in juxtaposition. They are brought together also in 12:23–37, where the worst of all slanders against

Jesus, that he works by the prince of demons, uttered by people 'against' Christ, 'blaspheming' the Son of man, is set in contrast with his 'amazing' power, his possession of the Spirit, and his warning of divine judgement upon what men say of him.

It is even *possible* that this paradox explains the strange words about blasphemy against the Son of man (in his humiliation) being forgivable, whereas blasphemy against the Spirit (when the Son of man is glorified and speaks by the Spirit?) will not be forgiven in this age or the age to come. But the passage is very obscure.

By thus setting majesty and humiliation side by side, Matthew makes plain that the contrast in the Servant-Messiah is true to fact, and no mere inconsistency in the telling.

But what emerges clearly from this dual portrait of Christ is the truth that we must see him—so to speak—*in process*, as passing through two or three phases. Even on earth, Christ carries his majesty through humiliation, willingly accepted. But the day comes when he is seen in very different light. The glory of the transfiguration is a foretaste of that; the promise of the resurrection is its guarantee. Jesus tells the high priest at his trial of these contrasted times: of the Christ he already sees before him, and the Son of man in glory that he shall yet see. In the resurrection stories this promise is fulfilled, as Jesus is seen clothed with 'all authority in heaven and on earth'. The church therefore already knows her Master in two phases—in the lowliness of his lifetime and in the risen, ascended exaltation of the church-time.

And the process of revelation cannot end there. The end-time beyond the church-time will see the Son of man coming 'with his angels in the glory of his Father . . . coming in his kingdom'; acknowledging his own before the Father in heaven, returning in an hour we do not know to take account with servants, arriving as a Bridegroom for the wedding feast, being hailed with 'Blessed is he who comes in the name of the Lord'. 'The sign of the Son of man' will appear in heaven, and all the tribes of the earth will mourn; they will see the Son of man coming on the clouds of heaven with power and great glory, and he will send out his angels with a loud trumpet call to gather his elect from the four winds and from one end of heaven to the other. It may be that 'the Lord is delayed', but before all is done the Master will come and the whole process of revelation reach its climax in a final unveiling of Messiah's glory.

Humiliation, majesty, glory: Matthew's certainty that the Master comes, that victory and glory lie ahead, rests not simply upon confident faith; not even upon remembered words of Jesus, taken alone; but upon the whole logic of the self-manifestation of the Servant-Messiah. The humiliation was only a stage: even the 'transfiguration' witnessed by the privileged few who saw him 'with eyes majestic after death' was only a stage: he will yet be seen by the world at large, even by those responsible for his death. As he himself had said to the Sanhedrin, 'I tell you, hereafter you will see the Son of man seated on the right hand of Power and coming on the clouds of heaven'. It is *necessary* that Christ should come again, to complete his work, to perfect our knowledge of himself. Past and present in the Christian story are wonderful but unfinished—incomplete—until he come.

Matthew's prescription for disappointment adds to this strong certainty a reasoned call for watchfulness. Matthew did not know any more than we know just *how*, in what form, or *when*, the end will come. That the future belongs to Christ, that destiny is Christ's to unfold, that the reins of history will be seen in the end to lie in his hands, all this Matthew understands: but not the manner or the time of the end. Nor, he says, does anyone else know (24:36). But whereas *we* make ignorance of the details, and the difficulty of imagining the advent, a reason for scepticism and unreadiness, and sometimes for a pose of superior agnosticism about the future, *Matthew*, with deeper spiritual wisdom, made ignorance a reason for alertness, for expectation, for open-mindedness toward the unforeseeable:

'But of that day and hour *no-one knows*, not even the angels of heaven, nor the Son, but the Father only. As were the days of Noah, so will be the coming of the Son of man. For as in those days before the flood they were eating and drinking, marrying and giving in marriage, until the day when Noah entered the ark, and *they did not know* until the flood came and swept them all away, so will be the coming of the Son of man. Then two men will be in the field: one is taken and one is left. Two women will be grinding at the mill; one is taken and one is left. Watch therefore for *you do not know* on what day your Lord is coming.

But *know this*, that *if the householder had known* in what part of the night the thief was coming, he would have watched and would not have let his house be broken into. Therefore you also must be ready: for the Son of man is coming at an hour *you do not expect.* . . . Watch therefore, *for you know neither the day nor the hour*' (24:36–44, 25:13).

But Matthew's spiritual wisdom was learned at the feet of Christ.

In the light of this strategy, that ignorance prompts alertness, it may be that all the charts and plans and programmes of the future laboriously constructed by devotees of prophecy have an opposite effect to that which zealous adventists intend. The assumption that in order to make the promises real you must be able to foresee the details is mistaken, and approaches the matter the wrong way. For it suggests that we live in an orderly, predictable world, in which even the future is regularised, blue-printed, pre-packed in prophetic verses, predetermined by unalterable laws, so that all we have to do is to sit back and watch the reel unwind. In contrast, the Christian view, Matthew's view, is that we live among miracles in an unpredictable world, with God about us all our days and the future wide open all the time. Matthew's adventism has that exciting quality: you *do not know* what will happen—so watch, all the time.

For all that, Matthew's idea of advent-preparation is not restless idleness, so sure of final victory that it does nothing at all to achieve it or bring it nearer. Listen once more to Matthew's great metaphors recalled from Jesus, describing Christian behaviour for 'meantime': faithful service as stewards in the Lord's absence; shining lamps well provided for all-night burning; trading in the world's markets with the Lord's entrusted gifts to bring him profit; feeding the hungry, clothing the naked, visiting the sick and the prisoner, as we would feed and clothe and visit him, caring for men as we care about him. And doing all in the same confidence that so the future is *made*; that so we are both preparing and being prepared, for the unforeseeable good which God has planned for those who love him. Doing all, too, in the sure hope that he that endures to the end will be saved, and the arriving King will say, 'Come, O blessed of my Father, inherit the kingdom. . . .'

CHAPTER TEN

The Church in society

Keeping still very close to what Matthew has written, and especially observing his 'editorial' additions and alterations as he borrows from Mark, we must take note of another curious paradox which is revealed in Matthew's attitude towards the first disciples.

Mark, we remember, shows no great tenderness, or even much respect, towards the Twelve. He records their brusque question to Jesus, '*Carest Thou* not that we perish?' and their almost impolite 'Shall we go and buy two hundred denarius' worth of bread for all these?' Matthew simply omits such rudeness. Mark tells of Jesus' sharp questions to the Twelve: 'Do you not understand? How will you understand anything?', which Matthew again omits. At a further point, the question 'Do you not understand?' is answered (in *Matthew* only) by 'Yes, we do'. And a third time (16:12) Matthew actually substitutes 'then they understood'.

'Why are you afraid?' 'Have you no faith?' with hard statements like Christ's indignation with the disciples for their sending away the children, their being amazed and afraid, their not understanding and being afraid to ask him; and the further sharp questions 'Do you not perceive or understand?'

'Are your hearts hardened?' 'Having eyes do you not see, and having ears do you not hear? And do you not remember?' all this Matthew either omits, when he comes upon it in *Mark*, or he tones it down. He leaves out, too, Peter's 'not knowing what to say' (perhaps Matthew just could not believe that!). And where Mark (6:52) has again 'they did not understand . . . their hearts were hardened', Matthew in telling the same story ends with 'Those in the boat worshipped him, saying, "Truly you are the Son of God".'

Fourteen instances of this softening revision of *Mark* by Matthew have been counted. But these are sufficient to show how much more considerate Matthew is, in general, for the character and reputation of the Twelve; how much gentler with their personal failings, their slowness in comprehending Jesus. Yet that is only one side of Matthew's picture of the earliest disciples.

Failure

For at the same time Matthew appears to emphasise deliberately the repeated failure of the disciples at certain key points in the story, actually underlining what Mark there says. At the foot of the mount of transfiguration a distressed father awaited healing for his 'possessed' epileptic boy. To notice exactly how Mark tells it, and then how Matthew alters *Mark*, is quite startling.

Mark gives the story some thirty-two lines, of which *one* reports the failure of the nine disciples to help, and *three* lines tell of their question to Jesus about this, and of his reply. The rest of Mark's space and all his emphasis are given to the suffering boy, the father's distress, and his piteous pleading. Matthew reduces the thirty-two lines to *fifteen*, cutting down the description of the suffering, omitting the father's moving plea and also the second demonic attack: yet he makes room for *six* lines of conversation about the disciples' failure. Over a third of Matthew's story is given to this, compared with one-eighth of Mark's.

Nor is that all. In *Mark*, Jesus answers the crowd's arguing, and the father's blunt words, 'I asked your disciples and they were not able' with words that trouble all of us: 'O faithless generation, how long am I to be with you? How long am I to bear with you?' We are left to puzzle over whether it is the father's despair, the attitude of the crowd, or the disciples' failure that is so sharply rebuked. In *Matthew*, all is clear. For the crowd have not opened their mouths, and the father has only made his simple request for help; there is no one, in Matthew's account, to whom the shattering rebuke *can* apply except the disciples—the faithless, powerless, disciples. All Matthew's attention is on them.

Equally instructive is Matthew's version of the story which Mark records in his chapter 6 of the stilling of a storm. Mark tells it in *fourteen* lines, all factual: the disciples are distressed in rowing because of the wind; Jesus comes walking on the sea; they saw him and were terrified, but immediately he spoke, and all was well. The disciples were astounded, but 'did not understand about the loaves because their hearts were hardened'. Matthew expands this by half as much again. He mentions their distance from the shore, the great waves, and (twice) the fear of the disciples. He says that they not only *thought* that Jesus was a ghost (as Mark said) but they *shouted* it, suggesting something of panic. Jesus spoke to them, and—this Matthew adds—

> 'Peter answered him, "Lord, if it is you, bid me come to you on the water". He said, "Come". So Peter got out of the boat and walked on the water and came to Jesus; but when he saw the wind, he was afraid, and beginning to sink he cried out, "Lord, save me". Jesus immediately reached out his hand and caught him, saying to him, "O man of little faith, why did you doubt?" And when they got into the boat, the wind ceased. . . .'

All the conversation and the space-walk was during the storm, which ends as the story closes: 'And those in the boat worshipped him, saying, "Truly you are the Son of God".'

In this instance, then, Matthew greatly lengthens Mark's story, but still in such a way as to concentrate upon Jesus and the Twelve, and especially upon Peter's *attempting to do what Jesus did*, and failing, until he cried out to Jesus. The storm, the danger, and the miracle fade into the background, almost as afterthoughts, while Matthew underlines Peter's failure and its outcome.

Matthew alters Mark's other storm-story (in *Mark* 4) also, and in a curious way. In *Mark*, Jesus is awakened by the rough question of the disciples, 'Carest Thou not . . .?' He first stills the storm, and then asks why they feared, adding 'Have you *no* faith?' In *Matthew*, when Jesus is wakened by the gentler plea, 'Save Lord, we are perishing', he first asks why they fear, speaking of their *little* faith. Then he arose and rebuked the wind. The change is not great, but it cannot be accidental; the effect is that in *Mark no faith* receives a miracle, and then reassurance: in *Matthew*, *little faith* receives assurance in the midst of the storm, and then a miracle. It is again failure—the disciples' failure to keep calm in the midst of storm—that Matthew emphasises.

A fourth instance is more debatable, but may be significant. Mark tells of the feeding of the five thousand in some nineteen lines; Matthew shortens this by a third, omitting the saying about seeing the crowd as sheep without a shepherd, the reference to the day's teaching, the grouping of the people upon the grass; he also twice omits any reference to the fish, a possibly important detail. For Matthew is not merely abbreviating: he adds the women and children and he adds another phrase, quite short, but for which he must have had a purpose. Where Mark says that Jesus gave to the disciples to give to the crowd (in seven words), Matthew says that he gave the loaves to the disciples and the disciples gave to the crowds (in eleven words) which, again, is possibly significant. Add to these two details the language about lifting up his eyes, blessing the bread, breaking it, and giving it to the disciples, who gave it to the people, and one immediately recalls the Lord's Supper, where there was no fish. It is but suggestion: yet such as it is, it spotlights the disciples and their special mediation in taking from Christ and giving to the people.

But if we look again at the beginning of the story,

we find that Mark shows the disciples suggesting that the crowd be sent to buy food, and Jesus replying, 'You give them something'. They retort with that bold counter-objection about buying two hundred denarius' worth of bread, dismissing so impractical a command, plainly not realising that Jesus will do the supplying. So Mark himself says later, 'they did not understand about loaves because their hearts were hardened'. Matthew has none of this. In reply to the disciples' suggestion, Matthew shows Jesus making the definite statement, 'They need not go away' which disposes of all objections from the start. But no objection is mentioned: all that the disciples say is, 'We have only five loaves here, and two fish'. Thus in *Mark*, they make objection, failing to understand; in *Matthew* they understand all right, but lack resources. Once again the disciples fail in the moment of need.

Such is the paradox of Matthew's attitude to the Twelve: on the one hand showing great respect for them, even reverence, and toning down their utterances and criticism of them; on the other hand, frankly acknowledging their helplessness, fear, failure and inadequacy. And in all four instances, Matthew deliberately adds to Mark's account in order to make this clear. One further remark seems justified, as one thinks of Matthew recording the stories *in this way* for his own congregation and his own time. The world continued hungry for life-giving bread, and Christians stood wringing their hands with little in store. Storms beat still upon the church in a hostile world, and Christian hearts were fearful and sinking. Society remained bedevilled by all forms of evil, lust, violence, and Christians cannot

124

cast them out. The instances seem remarkably relevant as illustrations of the church's continuing powerlessness to help society with its timeless and pressing problems.

Did Matthew intend to point that lesson?

Faith

If we stay a little longer with these failure stories, another side-light upon Matthew's mind gleams through.

When Matthew tells of the epileptic boy, focusing all attention on the disciples' failure and their conversation with Jesus about that, the rebuke which he records expressly calls them 'faithless'; while Christ's answer to the question why they failed, is 'because of your little faith'. To that are added two further sayings: one about faith as small as a grain of mustard seed being able to remove mountains; the other declaring that nothing is impossible to faith. Since nothing at all has been said (in Matthew) about the father's or the boy's faith, but only of the disciples' want of faith, these comments also must apply to the disciples' faith—lack of it explaining failure, but when they attain even a little, all will become possible.

In the storm stories the implication is similar. Peter's failure earns the rebuke 'O man of little faith, why did you doubt?' In the other story, the whole company are asked, 'Why are you afraid, O men of little faith?' Faith is not named in the story of the feeding of the five thousand, but the same comment is implied: at the beginning the disciples confess their inadequacy; at the end they are receiving from Jesus to distribute to the crowd—

which is the whole function of faith in the service of others.

We must not miss here the very rare word which Matthew uses to translate Christ's expression. It is found elsewhere only in *Luke* (once) and two or possibly three times in later Christian writings: *little-faith*.

> The epithet sounds like one of Bunyan's inventions, similar to 'Mr Valiant-for-Truth' but this name Bunyan actually borrows from Matthew. Mr Little-faith fell among thieves, lost his spending-money, and went doleful and complaining on his way, but he maintained his pilgrimage. As we might expect, Bunyan links Mr Little-faith with recollections of Peter, who 'upon a time would go try what he could do, but . . . they (Faint-heart, Mistrust) handled him so that they made him at last afraid of a sorry girl'.

Matthew uses 'little-faith' five times, always of the disciples, as they fail to heal, are afraid of the storm, fail to walk the waves, complain they have no bread (16:8), are anxious over clothes and food (6:30). The point Matthew is making could scarcely be clearer or more simple: the disciples understand very well, they are not so slow or confused as (reading *Mark*) we might think; but they do *lack power* in facing some situations in society, and their failures are through 'little-faith'.

If we turn from failure stories to great moments of success, we find Matthew constructing the same argument the opposite way. Mark tells of a woman pressing through the crowd, touching Jesus, and finding healing; Jesus asked who touched him, and the disciples protest at such a question. The woman, nevertheless, tells Jesus what had happened, and Jesus replies 'Your faith has made you well. . . .' In Matthew's account, much of this disappears; the crowd, the disciples, the question and the protest; all that remains is Jesus talking to the woman, about faith, before anything else happens; then the miracle occurs, and is dismissed very briefly with 'Instantly the woman was made well'.

Mark's account of the raising of the daughter of Jairus contains many vivid details: the request, 'My daughter is *dying*'; a most dramatic atmosphere; three disciples allowed to witness the miracle along with the parents; the Aramaic words of power, carefully preserved, 'Talitha, cumi'; and we see the child eating afterwards. Matthew severely condenses the story, ignoring all this. The request becomes more audacious, 'My daughter *has just died*, but come and lay your hand on her and she will live'. As Jesus reaches the house he is laughed at for suggesting that the girl is but 'sleeping', but he raises her. Matthew's omissions and changes all suggest that the crucial point of the incident was the daring request and the astonishing result. Such faith as that cannot fail. Two verses later, Jesus himself voices the comment, 'According to your faith be it done to you'.

Mark does not relate the healing of the centurion's 'boy' but Matthew thought it well to preserve it for his church. We can compare Matthew's version with Luke's, and at once notice that Matthew omits the deputation of elders who testify that the soldier is *worthy* to receive help; we notice, too, that the single reference to the man's faith (in Luke's story) becomes in *Matthew* a four-fold comment, on the absence of faith where one would expect it ('no, not in Israel'); on the exceptional quality of such faith ('he marvelled . . . such faith'); on the wide scope of the results to be expected when Gentiles thus find faith ('many will come from the east and west and sit at table with Abraham, Isaac, and Jacob in the kingdom of heaven'); and on the explanation of the whole event ('be it done for you as you have had faith').

Once more: Mark tells of Jesus seeking retirement on the borders of Phoenicia, where a native woman asks healing for her daughter. Jesus objects that the children must first be fed, before the 'dogs', but the woman makes the clever reply that house-dogs may eat the crumbs that fall from the children's table. Jesus approves, and assures the woman that her daughter is healed, and so she finds on reaching home. Matthew again makes significant alterations: he shows Jesus silent to the woman, and the disciples asking that she be sent away; Jesus then speaks to the disciples about the lost sheep of Israel, but the woman asks again, and the *unfairness* of giving the children's food to dogs is then mentioned. On hearing her clever reply, Jesus exclaims (in Matthew only) 'O woman, great is your faith! be it done for you as you desire', and her daughter was healed. Matthew leaves no doubt that the climax of the story lay in that exclamation: it was the faith of the woman that overcame the reluctance of Jesus.

Both these 'Gentile' miracles have especial importance. Mark makes the point about 'Jews *first*' which was also Paul's reply when Judaists objected to a mission among Gentiles: 'to the Jew first, and then to the Gentiles' (so in *Romans* 1:16; 11:11; *Acts* 28:25–28). Matthew, however, insists that both the centurion and the Syro-Phoenician have *faith*, nothing at all is said of who should have first opportunity. It is not priority of race, but the presence of faith, that brings salvation: that is the argument also of the Jerusalem Council on this subject: God 'cleansing their hearts by faith', the church must accept them into membership. Thus the apostolic church had two arguments for admitting Gentiles: Mark gives one, Matthew the other; and Matthew's is his favourite theme, 'According to your faith. . . .'

To these specially illuminating examples we can again add repetition of a characteristic phrase. Four times Matthew records 'According to your faith be it done to you . . .' (or) 'Your faith has saved you'. There are thirteen other instances where Matthew emphasises the role of faith in the miracle stories: for example, it was 'when Jesus saw their faith' that he healed the paralytic; his first word to the blind men was 'Do you believe that I am able to do this?'; the disciples' surprise at the fig-tree's withering was met by 'If you have faith and never doubt' you will do more. Of course Matthew did not invent this theme, for it rests on words of Jesus and the other Gospels refer to it. But Matthew underlines it firmly, sometimes adjusting his narratives to make it central.

Here then are eight stories, one phrase used five times and another four times, plus other instances, all saying, first negatively and then positively, that the secret of power is faith. On the one side, the disciples understood, but lacking faith they failed at moments of need; on the other side, the disciples witnessed great deeds, and the power they saw at work was always mediated through faith. Matthew wanted his church to remember that. Power, and powerlessness, are matters of *faith*.

What is faith?

When we hear Matthew say about his church, and when we imply about the churches we know, that all spiritual ineffectiveness, frustration, inability to save society, ineptness in organisation, incompetence in evangelism, lack of authority in preaching and of persuasiveness in counselling, are due to one cause—want of *faith*—it is well to be quite clear what we mean by faith: otherwise we are guilty of mindless diagnosis, glib prescription, and quite irresponsible jargon-mongering. What is this faith which we pretend would, if we possessed it, yield us power?

The question is not trite or superfluous. To Paul in *Romans* faith is union with Christ in his death and risen life; faith means being 'in Christ'. In the Pastoral Epistles faith is nearer to orthodoxy in doctrine. To John faith is 'a kind of seeing', grasping the full meaning of Christ's coming and death, an insight into divine truth such as brings eternal life. To Luke faith is acceptance of the gospel, so that its promises come true to those who live by it. In *Hebrews* (11) faith is the vision of the unseen, living by invisible directions and resources. James regards faith, without works, as merely intellectual, something that the devils share in. Peter prefers to speak of love for Christ, though that includes a clear estimate of who he is. Such differences of emphasis illustrate the central place of faith in Christianity, and the care needed in comparing what different New Testament writers say.

Matthew does not mean precisely faith in the gospel, nor the 'saving faith' which brings a man into relationship with Christ. As we shall see Matthew's description of 'conversion' is somewhat different; the want of faith of which he speaks is not *unbelief* or rejection of Christ; the men of little faith are nevertheless disciples. Certainly there is in Matthew's 'faith' an element of trust and confidence, the very word implies that. Yet it is not 'a state of heart' either, not something going on inside ourselves, a psychological preparation or conditioning for power. Nor, for all his insistence upon Christian righteousness, does Matthew ever suggest that it is by our own merit, by way of reward for our consecration of character or dedication of life, that God grants us power for our service. Equally clearly Matthew never suggests that faith itself is power, an attitude of mind releasing hidden psychological resources. There is no such phrase in the New Testament as 'the power of faith'.

For Matthew faith is always *expressed* in some way, and not simply felt. It is shown by a woman's reaching out her hand to touch Jesus; by four friends carrying the paralytic to Christ; by the blind calling after Jesus in the street; by Peter stepping out upon the water. It is faith made visible and audible: even the shy woman with an 'unmentionable' illness was not allowed to keep her healing wholly secret. Faith, in *Matthew*, must be expressed in wonder, or in worship, in an acted request, in grasping after Christ, in a laying hold of, against all obstacles, the source of power.

There are obstacles: crowds to press through, distance to overcome, Gentile barriers to break down, death to defy; but to Matthew, faith is energetic, importunate, active, never passive or pietistic. At certain points Matthew suggests that faith resembles *willing* a thing to happen: 'O woman, great is your faith! Be it done for you as you desire' and 'So be it done for you as you have believed'. Both seem to assume that the *faith* and the *will* or the *desire*, are the same attitude of soul, or that faith is a form of volition. Not that faith is a force within ourselves creating a miracle (it should be said again), but rather that faith is a plea towards something outside ourselves, to which the miracle is the answer.

Faith is active, energetic, often unspoken, prayer; power is the divine reply. The forceful, adventuring, enterprising trust that lays hold upon power, counts upon it without doubting, that is 'great faith', in the centurion, in the paralytic's friends, in the shy woman, the Syro-Phoenician mother, the blind men—*but not in the disciples*! Not one of the persons commended for faith, in Matthew's Gospel, is an apostle.

Because as Matthew saw the disciples, both in Christ's time and now in his own time, they lacked the faith that liberates power. Theirs was 'little-faith', broken faith, half-faith, intermittent faith perhaps, minimal faith as it might be called, faith mixed (some moderns would pretend) 'with a healthy dose of agnosticism'; faith touched with 'realism', playing with scepticism in order to appear 'reasonable' and 'adult'. That gets disciples nowhere: the possessed go unexorcised, the hungry wait unfed, Christians lose their nerve in the world's wild storm. In a world like ours, faith that is a mere balance of probabilities, a wistful half-belief that evades the challenge of the supernatural, compromising whenever possible with the materialistic scepticism of the modern world, must be powerless.

Such half-belief may be better than no faith at all, for in a curious way it is also a broken unbelief, lacking the conviction, or the courage, to cut loose and deny Christ. But for all that, it must be ineffectual, frustrated, useless, a prodding conscience without inspiration or joy, a wistful *wanting* to help others but having barely sufficient resources to handle its own problems. It will always be found standing helpless amid a jeering crowd, pleading 'Why could not we . . .?' Or timidly stepping out upon deep water and then faltering before the waves and the wind; or facing a hungry, demanding world and wistfully confessing 'We don't have what it takes'. For it must be admitted, of many of us who love Christ and follow the Christian way, that we have faith enough to make us disciples, but not enough to liberate power into lives around us.

Yet while Matthew's diagnosis finds us where we are, mere men of little-faith, it does not suffice for cure. Faith does not emerge of itself from some spiritual depths within the soul: it is created in us by

133

the gospel's offer of something infinitely worth believing in; it is a deliberate and complete dependence, evoked by the presentation to mind and heart of something entirely dependable. For the strength of faith lies not within itself, its feelings, constancy, depth, intensity; the strength of faith lies wholly in that to which it is directed, upon which it is focused, in which it rests. To what, then, does Matthew direct our little-faith, that it may become great faith?

Faith in what?
For the last time, let us watch how Matthew handles stories which he shares with Mark: Mark probably learned from Peter of that memorable sabbath when Jesus came with other disciples from the synagogue to Peter's home, to be told that his wife's mother had been stricken with fever; and how Jesus had taken her by the hand and raised her from her sick-bed, so swiftly well that she immediately ministered to the numerous company. When Matthew tells the story, the synagogue, disciples, (even Peter), and the others who tell Jesus of the need, all disappear: they are irrelevant. No-one receives attention in Matthew's version but Jesus and the patient—*he* saw the need; *he* touched her hand; she arose and served *him*. Matthew moves Christ to the centre of the story, since he only has the power that heals.

Watch how Matthew retells the story of the man of Gadara, on which Mark had dwelt so lovingly. Matthew drops the long description of the man's history and symptoms, and omits the desire of the man to leave his home and travel with the Twelve. Three things preoccupy Matthew: the cry of the

134

demons that Jesus is the Son of God with power to torture them; Jesus' authority to grant the plea of the demons that they might go into the swine and to bid them go; and the whole city and district streaming out to see, not the healed man (as Mark says) but *Jesus*, and to beg *him* to leave their neighbourhood. Matthew has moved Jesus to the centre of another story; only *he* has the power that drives out evil.

In telling of the healing of the paralytic, Mark has two equal themes, the claim to forgive sins, and the miracle which evoked the people's wonder. Matthew concentrates upon the claim to forgive; the miracle has place as proof of that claim. And Matthew's story ends, not with the man's actions and elation— Matthew merely says 'he rose and went home'— but with the crowd's *fear*, and their glorifying God for the authority given to men like Jesus. Matthew has moved Christ to the centre of that story, too, as alone having the right to pronounce pardon.

Once more, and to leave Matthew's method here beyond doubt, let us note how he changes Mark's stories of the stilling of the storms. In each, Matthew's point is not what Jesus does with the weather, but what he does with his men. Their relation to him is everything. In the one story, he first rebuked their panic 'Why are you afraid, O men of little faith?' In the other, he rebuked them for losing nerve amid the storm, calling as he strode through the darkness, 'Take heart, it is I; have no fear'. Then he bids Peter come to him across the waves and so long as Peter sees Jesus and not the storm, he succeeds, and succeeds again when Jesus reached a hand to him. All that told, Matthew remarks, in three words, 'the wind ceased'. *Matthew moves Christ to the centre of every story, because the power is in him.*

That is Matthew's answer to the church's powerlessness. But we miss the whole point if we fail to notice that Christ *intended* his power to be shared. That is the burden of the mission charge. Jesus 'gave them power' to share his experience, his authority, his work, his protection, and his vindication at the end. This, too, is the meaning of the promise at the healing of the epileptic: 'all things are possible' not to Christ only but to 'whoever believes'. Disciples *can* walk the waves, if they fix their eyes upon Christ and place their hand in his. The church's sinking ship can survive the storm once Christ is in command. Clearest instance of all, and very surprisingly, is when Matthew makes the healing of the paralytic end with the people marvelling that such authority was given not to *Jesus* but to *men*. For Christ, in whom all power dwells, intends that we shall share in it, by faith.

Here is the focus of faith for Matthew—the Christ of the miracle stories, the Lord with power over men's bodies, minds, and hearts, over nature and over demons and over death.

But by Matthew's time, the situation had changed. When the miracles happened and the promises were given, Christ was in humiliation, the obedient Servant, meek and lowly in heart. Then he would not strive or cry out in the streets; he was the king lowly upon an ass; men criticised, abused, betrayed him. Now, says Matthew, recalling other words of Christ, now he is not like that. He had promised earlier that where two or three gather in his name there he would be, in the midst of them. After Easter, on the eve of his ascension, he came clothed 'with all authority in heaven and on earth', the Lord-designate of the world, waiting for the end-time of his glory, the risen, ascending, exalted King, and repeated the promise, 'Lo, I am with you, always, to the close of the age'.

That is Matthew's complete prescription for powerlessness, and the little, broken, minimal faith that causes it: the Christ of the miracle stories, now the Christ of the resurrection and ascension, is *the Lord within the congregation*, not coming only but present now, one who should be at the centre of every Christian story. The faith that liberates power is faith in the ascended Lord, already resident in the midst of the church and soon to come in glory at the end.

Matthew, after all, chose to meet the needs of the church around him, not by writing an Epistle, expounding truth and ethics, but by writing a *Gospel*, pointing men back to what the Master said, and here especially to what the Master did, and promised we might do. The faith that shall empower the church to survive the world, and to serve the world, is faith in the wonder-working Jesus as he now is, the ever-present Christ. Matthew knew his fellow-members. Even on the hillside above Bethany, he recalls, when Christ appeared in power, there were some who 'doubted'. That is his comment on the church he knows. 'Lo, I am with you, always, to the end of the age' is Matthew's challenge, as it was Christ's, to the church: to rise to the height of her faith and lay hold of the power that waits in her risen, indwelling, Lord.

With that climactic, final promise, Matthew's Gospel ends: because there is, quite literally, nothing more to say. But unless the church hears it the world will remain hungry for life-giving bread; the storm will beat upon the church and Christian hearts be terrified; society will remain bedevilled by all forms of evil and Christians will wistfully seek explanations why they cannot cast them out. We owe it, not only to the Master but to a desperately needy age, to find again the power that was in Christ, and set it free to heal and save society.

CHAPTER ELEVEN

On being a disciple

The church in Matthew's time and in our own consists of individual disciples. Bound together in loyalty, sharing a common faith, a common worship, a common task and a common Lord, they remain individuals still, who came to discipleship singly, who owe a personal responsibility each to his own Master, and who will be called singly to give account of their stewardship. All that Matthew has said about the church, its deficiencies and its needs, must therefore, if it is to bear fruit, ring true in individual minds and lie upon individual consciences. Righteousness is an individual ideal, insofar as each soul must seek alignment with the will of God, and strive to obey the commandments of its Lord; even social righteousness has its roots in individual justice and compassion.

Love, the fulfilment of all law and the crown of righteousness, is an individual attitude. The final judgement, of which Matthew has said so much, is usually presented in terms of personal obligation and assessment; and the anticipation of Christ's coming is an inspiration for individual service. The faith that mediates power is shared, even contagious: yet in the ultimate analysis it, too, consists of an individual laying-hold of the living Christ.

In the end, therefore, all that Matthew has to teach is directed towards improving the quality of personal discipleship.

Becoming a disciple
Matthew offers no psychological analysis of the process of conversion, nor any theology of salvation. Discipleship begins with the call to repentance: Matthew represents that call as the very first announcement of Jesus in his proclamation of the kingdom. Such repentance is further described as a 'turning' or conversion into that child-likeness without which no-one ever enters the kingdom. To the question, 'Who is the greatest in the kingdom of heaven?' Jesus replied by defining the condition of entering the kingdom at all—with a child set in the midst of the disciples to make his answer memorable.

It is neither the helplessness, the innocence, nor the faith of children which is highlighted, but *humility* (18:4), which may be best understood (in such a context) as the natural unselfconsciousness of little children—to whom, when some delight is offered, personal worth, dignity, and questions of desert do not normally come to mind. The artificial, consciously cultivated 'humility' of adults is very different; only the truly humble heart can 'receive the kingdom as a little child' receives anything, as a free, unmerited favour, yet entirely without embarrassment, hurt pride, or injured self-importance.

Mark at this point (after the setting of the child in midst) merely records a saying about the right treatment of children; but later he tells of the children being brought to Jesus, adding the sayings 'Let the children come to me, do not hinder them; for to such belongs the kingdom of God. Truly I say to you, whoever does not receive the kingdom of God like a child shall not enter it'. Matthew appears to take the second of these sayings (at 18:3) to illustrate the particular quality of child-likeness which prepares for the kingdom ('of *such* is the kingdom'), namely humility; and to preserve the first of Mark's sayings at 19:13 in his much-abbreviated account of the bringing of the children to Jesus.

Matthew is very clear that for all adults such a spirit involves the total reversal of habitual attitudes; that is, it involves repentance, 'conversion', complete change: this could well be the foundation of the later Johannine doctrine of new birth into the kingdom (*John* 3:3). We shall see, however, that for Matthew 'conversion', though radical, is not a once-for-all experience. Repentance is not here further defined, except as requiring 'fruits' to prove its presence (3:8).

The process of becoming a disciple is demonstrated rather than analysed in the accounts of the first call to men to 'follow' Jesus. The call of disciples is shown as the very first act of the Messiah, following immediately the bare statement that he preached repentance and announced the kingdom. Here Matthew uses *Mark* almost without alteration, even strengthening Mark's clear emphasis upon the immediacy of their response: for where Mark says 'he immediately called them' Matthew alters it to 'he called . . . and they immediately followed'. It is striking, too, that the call is straightway to be fishers —a call to call others.

The only other call to discipleship recorded in *Matthew* is that of the man named Matthew 'sitting at the tax office'. It is recorded in two short sentences, the emphasis again falling upon the immediacy of the response. If the following feast was in Matthew's house and not in that of Jesus, then probably the objection raised to Christ's eating with tax collectors is a comment upon Matthew's call to discipleship. The reply of Jesus, 'those who are well have no need of a physician . . . I came not to call the righteous but sinners . . .' opens discipleship to all who are willing to come, whatever their past.

Becoming a disciple, then, requires a change of spirit to humble, unselfconscious receptiveness, and the outward evidence of it is an immediate, uncalculating, but active, response to the invitation of Jesus. If the implications of conversion are unfolded at all, it must be in the two basic attitudes assumed by Matthew in disciples: understanding of Jesus, and hunger for righteousness.

We saw that Matthew plays down Mark's criticisms of the disciples on several counts; but in avoiding Mark's strictures on one particular matter, the disciples' slowness or lack of understanding, more is implied than a wish to spare the reputation of the Twelve. Matthew is formulating discipleship itself a little differently. For him, understanding Jesus *constitutes* discipleship: 'faith in Christ' is a further stage—the appropriation of the power made available in Christ, in order to do his work.

Matthew makes seven alterations to *Mark* each implying this difference of terms, see p 119f above. Matthew does leave Mark's words 'not understanding' at one place, where it refers only to the disciples' difficulty over a particular saying of Jesus.

So, in describing the disciples' failures through lack of faith, Matthew has no doubt at all that they *are* disciples. Absence of faith does not (in Matthew's language) mean rejection of Christ, but insufficient trust. And they are disciples because the Father, who has hidden the things of the kingdom from the supposedly wise and prudent, has 'revealed them to babes' (11); because, like Peter, they have learned what flesh and blood could not reveal to them, but only the Father in heaven (16); because to them it has been given to know the secrets of the kingdom of heaven, and they receive private instruction 'in the house' from Jesus (13); because they have heard the sayings of Jesus, and seek to do them (7).

Thus, to have understood who Jesus is, to have understood the secrets of the kingdom and the sayings of the Master, is to be distinguished from the imperceptive multitude (13:13), and from the wilful Jewish authorities who choose not to understand. It implies therefore an inward relinquishing of the 'hardness of heart' which refuses to understand. To know the secrets of the kingdom is, nevertheless, an immense privilege *given* by the Father, and not something to boast about: 'Blessed are your eyes, for they see, and your ears for they hear. Truly, I say to you, many prophets and righteous men longed to see what you see, and did not see it, and to hear what you hear, and did not hear it'. The very word *disciple*, of course, carries this implication of growing understanding.

The other basic attitude of the disciple is the hunger for that righteousness which it is Messiah's purpose to establish on the earth. Disciples are essentially *those who do* the will of the Father, as that will—that higher righteousness—is interpreted in the sayings of Jesus, supremely as love of God and neighbour. This alone (as we saw) will guarantee Christ's acknowledgement at the end (7), and now constitutes kinship with Messiah (12). This *doing the will* is also taking Christ's 'yoke'—the yoke of his law and teaching—upon one's shoulders, learning of him; as it is also to seek the kingdom of God and his righteousness.

What this may cost the disciple is spelled out in several ways. It means doing something 'more than others'—the Gentiles, or the tax-gatherers: living above the average of one's society (5). It means excelling the scribes and Pharisees in the pursuit of righteousness.

This *may be* the meaning of 'being perfect' as your Father is perfect (the likelier meaning is, 'Be all-inclusive in your love as your Father is'). It is clearly the meaning of 'perfect' as spoken to the 'rich young ruler' who had asked 'What lack I yet?' These terms appear to have been current in Jewry in Christ's time; for the Qumran covenanters speak of those who keep the whole undiluted law as 'those who *do more*' or 'the *perfect*' just as Matthew does.

One key saying which well expresses this 'above the average' hungering and thirsting after righteousness is Christ's phrase 'But it shall not be so among you . . .'—what others do is not *your* standard! If the famous beatitudes were not by now so smoothly familiar as no longer to shock us, we would find them the most startling description of it, for they extol all the qualities which the world despises, and pronounce blessed in the kingdom all the attitudes which elsewhere lead to failure. The world's standards are simply irrelevant to those who would be disciples.

For some becoming a disciple will mean leaving behind, or giving away, great wealth, where possessions are the hindrance to commitment: though when Peter unguardedly boasted of how much the Twelve had given up for Christ, he was sharply and, surely ironically, reminded that God is no man's debtor.

The 'rich young ruler' having turned away at Christ's demand, and Jesus having commented that it will be hard for a rich man to enter the kingdom, the disciples 'greatly astonished' say 'Who then can be saved?' Jesus said it is possible with God, and Peter replied 'Lo, we have left everything and followed you. What then shall we have?' Jesus said to them 'Truly, I say to you, in the new world, when the Son of man shall sit on his glorious throne, you who have followed me will also sit on twelve thrones, judging the twelve tribes of Israel. And everyone who has left houses or brothers or sisters or father or mother or children or lands, for my name's sake, will receive

145

a hundredfold, and inherit eternal life. But many that are first will be last, and the last first.' (Even if such a promise of abundant material reward were *not* wholly out of harmony with the call to take up the cross, we could hardly take these words as a solemn, literal promise, since Judas is included).

For others, discipleship may well involve division from one's family, as Christ claims supreme place in the individual's love and loyalty (10). Another renunciation sometimes demanded is that of personal ambition, for the new way to greatness is by becoming servant of all, not seeking pre-eminence or power for oneself (20). For all, the higher righteousness will mean entering a narrow gate, walking an unpermissive way, lonely because few find it, though it leads to life (7).

If such a description of discipleship, as essentially understanding Christ and searching for righteousness appears strangely eccentric and unfamiliar, that merely shows how sorely modern Christians need Matthew's message.

Probationary discipleship
Still more strange, though, to many modern Christians, is Matthew's presentation of discipleship as a tentative trial stage, whose ultimate outcome is as yet in doubt. This is sufficiently epitomised in watchwords like 'many are called, but few are chosen'; 'many that are first shall be last'; and 'he that endures to the end shall be saved'. Each such saying leaves something uncertain, something yet to be decided. To be called 'to follow'

also implies, to some degree, that one has not yet arrived; and to those who 'hunger and thirst after righteousness' is expressly promised the *ultimate* reward of being 'satisfied' not a present attainment. Disciples do not yet 'shine as the sun in the kingdom of the Father'.

A hint of the same truth seems implied in the existence of grades among the Twelve. Four are introduced by an account of their call; one more is added in the same way; later three emerge as specially privileged or trusted (at the transfiguration and in the garden of Gethsemane; Mark adds at the house of Jairus). Peter especially is awarded prominence both by commendation and by promised responsibility. To be a disciple, it appears, was not in any sense to have reached finality: one was 'on the way' and no more than that.

The word 'disciple' likewise implies incompleteness, and it is striking that the title remains right up to Matthew's time in his circle, the usual description of Christians. They *remain* learners, to the earthly end, a church of learners; although it is given to them to understand, they still must hear the call 'Come . . . learn of me . . .' (11). This concept of a 'school' of learners around a teacher was borrowed from Judaism, though it was known more widely in the philosophic 'schools' of Greece. But it must be noticed that in contrast to usage in Jewish and Greek disciple-groups, the disciples around Jesus do not discuss ideas with him (in the fashion, for example, of the Socratic Dialogues); nor is it imagined that the disciples become the successors of the teacher. Matthew hints at this difference of relationship, by showing that though others may call Jesus

147

teacher, rabbi, disciples always use the title 'Lord'.

Matthew says much about Christ's 'little ones'. The child in the midst of the Twelve (18) was a literal child: but the following sayings concern 'little ones who believe in me' and who (as Matthew has set the parable in *his* context) are also 'sheep'— church members—who need especial care, a well-organised procedure of reconciliation when they give offence to the brethren, and an endless forgiveness. These, too, are the 'babes' to whom the gracious Father has revealed the divine truth. In this metaphor of 'little ones' it is the helplessness, vulnerability and lowliness of the children/sheep that seem to be in mind; as in the beatitudes it is 'poverty of spirit', hunger, mourning, 'the being empty before God' which receives the comforting promise. Disciples do not outgrow their utter dependence on the seeking Shepherd and the loving Lord: they are never, in Matthew, able 'to go it alone'. At the consummation of all things they will be called 'the righteous . . . the elect . . . the blessed of the Father', but not yet.

This probationary tentativeness that marks discipleship in Matthew becomes more disturbing in three particular directions. Firstly, Matthew appears to think of conversion as a continuing or at least a developing experience. For the reminder of the necessity to be 'converted' to the child-spirit comes fourteen chapters *after* the first call to discipleship; and yet another new stage appears to be reached when, after Peter's confession at Caesarea Philippi, Jesus begins to forecast his own death, and to speak of the need that the disciples also shall take up the cross. Both Mark and Luke note clearly the same profound change in the message, language, and mood of Jesus as he turns his face toward Jerusalem; but only Matthew expresses it in the form *spoken to the disciples* 'if any man *would* come after me, let him deny himself and take up his cross and follow me'. What is implied here is plainly a revision of the terms of discipleship, and a call for fresh decisions.

Secondly, Matthew's thought of membership within the kingdom of heaven as not yet bestowed, while still the disciples 'seek first the kingdom' and wait to hear 'Come . . . inherit the kingdom . . .' itself implies a probationary discipleship. As we have seen, there are expressions in Matthew which suggest that the kingdom is ever at hand, and can be already experienced in some measure; but the verdict at the coming judgement will be for final admission or exclusion: *possession* of the kingdom is yet to be decided. *Then* will the kingdom be purged of evil, and the righteous shine: until then all is provisional, preparatory.

Thirdly, and yet more disturbing, Matthew has a sixfold reference to the possibility of being repudiated by Jesus in the end. To those who merely professed the lordship of Christ, 'I never knew you . . . depart from me'; 'whoever denies me before men, I also will deny before the Father . . .'; 'the master of that *servant* will come . . . and will punish him and put him with the hypocrites . . .'; the Bride-groom replied, 'Truly, I say to you, I do not know you . . .' ('Watch therefore . . .' is the added warning *to Matthew's readers*); the worthless *servant* is cast into outer darkness; the goats within the flock are told to 'Depart . . .' Add to these warnings the

Master's words, recalled for Matthew's church, about the kingdom being taken from those who possess it and given to others, and the possibility of God's withdrawing forgiveness from the unforgiving, and Matthew's stern intention is plain.

He leaves no room for doubt that present discipleship is probationary; there is a sifting ahead, and 'Every plant which my heavenly Father has not planted will be rooted up' (15:13, spoken of Pharisees at first, now repeated to the church; and notice 'every'). Matthew desires his fellow-members within the church to take much more seriously the danger of personal failure, as well as of social powerlessness. For none can safely presume upon the goodness or the patience of God.

This austere representation of discipleship appears to contradict the absolute assurances of Paul and of John, that there is no condemnation for those in Christ Jesus; that those who have the Son have life, and shall not come into condemnation. But all such assurances presuppose sincerity of faith and purpose, though not of course infallibility or sinlessness. Even the great promise that 'nothing shall separate us from the love of God . . .' does not deny that we can separate ourselves. Always, along with such assurances that only *we* can defeat God's loving purpose in our lives. there are given warnings that such can happen: 'Let him that thinks he stands take heed lest he fall. . . . We must all appear before the judgement seat of Christ. . . . It is impossible to restore again to repentance those who have once been enlightened, who have tasted of the heavenly gift, and have become partakers of the Holy Spirit, and have tasted the goodness of the word of God and the powers of the age to come, if they then commit apostasy. . . . If we sin deliberately after receiving knowledge of the truth, there no longer remains a sacrifice for sins, but a fearful prospect of judgement . . .' The author of *Hebrews*, like the author of *Matthew*, has lived long enough to see the need of such warnings, when Christianity has become nominal, and Christian assurance is too easily assumed by half-committed 'believers'.

Discipleship that counts

Drawing together the qualities of discipleship that Matthew has mainly emphasised, we notice first that he regards the call to be a disciple as a call not so much to shared spiritual experiences or to 'blessing', as a call to witness, to work, to mission. The original call to be 'fishers of men' is repeated in the call to be 'apostles'; for where Mark says that the appointment as apostles was for *two* purposes, 'that they might be with him and that he might send them forth to preach', Matthew mentions only the second, the appointment to mission. Similarly, in *Matthew* the only reference to any instruction of the disciples refers to the charge preparatory to the Galilean mission.

Again, the disciple is not to hide his light under a flour-measure: he is to let his light so shine before men that they may see his good works and give glory to the Father in heaven. The disciple-band is set in a dark world like a city on a hill-top whose lighted windows cannot be hid. Perhaps in the increasing tension between church and synagogue, and the divisions within families that resulted from (actual or threatened) exclusion of Christians from Judaism, the temptation to hide discipleship, or even to deny Christ, was greater than ever. Pressures of patriotism, religious tradition, domestic loyalty, and inner uncertainty, may be harder to face than physical danger.

Whatever the reason, Matthew sharpens the demand of discipleship for confession of faith, for public commitment to Christ, for mission to one's own people and to the world. Mark and Luke share the warning of Jesus that whoever denies him before men, he will deny before the Father in heaven: but both leave it in that negative form, and by adding 'when he comes in the glory of his Father with the holy angels', they push the danger away to the end of time. Matthew adds the positive promise, 'Everyone who acknowledges me before men I also will acknowledge before my Father who is in heaven . . .'; and he leaves both promise and warning *timeless*. Not only at the end, but now and always, the ascended Christ acknowledges before God as his own those who bravely witness for him amid the perils of a hostile world.

Yet there is warning, and dreadful warning, in Matthew. After describing in detail the denial of Jesus by Peter, following the solemn forecast of it by Jesus and Peter's equally solemn affirmation of his readiness to die for Jesus, and sparing nothing of vividness in narrating Peter's repeated fall and violent language, Matthew is the only Gospel writer who states, curtly, 'he went out, and wept bitterly' *and never mentions Peter again.* (*Luke* restores

Peter to favour, in his second volume; *John* does so in what appears to be an appendix; *Matthew* not at all). Matthew's readers could scarcely miss the significance of that!

Matthew also assigns large place in discipleship to *sharing with* Christ. In the mission charge, Christ's men are called to share his work, authority, rejection and vindication, while 'A disciple is not above his teacher nor a servant above his master; it is enough for the disciple to be like his teacher and the servant like his master'. This theme is pursued in the full discussion of how the disciples may share his power by their faith; and share his secrets of the kingdom. It reaches a new intensity with the call to take up the cross, as Jesus does, and still follow. Sharing his sorrow and sharing his glory are placed side by side (16:24–28).

A share in the experience of the transfiguration was allowed to three; to all it is repeated that the way to greatness is through service, 'even as the Son of man came not to be served but to serve and to give his life a ransom for many'. So disciples are called to humility, as he is 'meek and lowly in heart'. In private conversation on the Mount of Olives, disciples share his vision of the future, and then by his arrangement the final evening meal with its deep undertones of Passover, covenant, sorrow and hope. Only some are privileged to share the intense agony of the garden of Gethsemane, but all experience the shock of his arrest. In the final scene, they still share in his universal authority, and go forth to his work with him beside them.

All this may fairly be described as 'the inner side' of discipleship. It comprised a 'growing together' between Christ and the one who seeks to follow him, in which the sharing of the Master's experiences, responsibilities, sufferings and glory is closely linked to sharing also the Master's mind (through his teaching), his attitudes, reactions, and faith. It would be hard to distinguish here *sharing* from *imitation*: and it is unnecessary. To watch through Matthew's eyes, the disciples' growing in understanding and attachment to their Master, giving up all other interests and securities, striving to grow to his mind and share his vision, suffering, and mission, and all out of love that is never (in Matthew) spoken about but is certainly there, is to learn what Matthew would consider discipleship worthy of the Lord.

For the rest, we need recall only briefly Matthew's larger themes. Hearing Christ's sayings, as he interprets God's law and expounds the fulfilment of all righteousness in the rule of love; waiting in fear, service, and hope, for the end-time of judgement and glory; laying hold, by active faith, of the power that is in Christ, in the midst of the congregation, so as to serve the world in its diverse need—all this is discipleship. For Matthew knew as we do, that the work of Christ in the world will not be done until the church discovers again her conscience and her power; and she cannot do that except as individual hearts hear once again the call to a discipleship that counts.

CHAPTER TWELVE

The mind of Matthew

Our quest was to catch Matthew's personal view-point as he retold the story of Jesus, to discern his mind and practical purpose. We assumed that as a leading teacher in the church, with Mark's account already in his hands, Matthew was doing what every preacher does when he uses the words and deeds of Jesus to draw contemporary lessons for his hearers. This cannot be *proved*: but we saw that even if such deliberate use and editing of *Mark* and of existing traditions about Jesus be denied, the differences between *Matthew*, *Mark* and *Luke* would still remain, and would demand some likelier explanation. The portrait that emerges from this description of Matthew's work is that of a skilled and ardent apologist for the Christian faith, who is also a devoted and very courageous pastor of the Christian church.

The mind of the advocate

The skill is that of an advocate, a barrister or counsel, marshalling arguments, meeting opposition, persuading for a verdict; the ardour is that of an evangelist, whose aim is commitment to Christ as King and Teacher, Saviour and Lord. For Matthew contrives so to tell the story as to leave no doubt that

Jesus is the Christ, the utterly righteous one, who has come to establish God's rule, righteousness, and judgement, in God's own world.

From his introduction of Jesus as supernaturally born of Davidic descent, his experience parallel in many respects to that of ancient Israel, his coming announced by the latest of the prophets, to his suffering and death in obedience to the divine will and in accord with age-old prophecy, Matthew builds up 'a massive argument for the kingship of Jesus'. At every point Matthew emphasises Christ's fulfilment of Old Testament scripture, the signs of his prophetic commission, his unswerving righteousness from baptism to death, his messianic authority in word, as with masterly clarity he interprets the divine law, and in deed, as he heals the sick, expels demons, and controls nature.

Matthew's case is unanswerable. In the days when church and synagogue were at long last finally severing relationships, Matthew made a strong effort to persuade his fellow Jews of the truth about Jesus. Alongside trenchant criticism of those tendencies within Jewry which led an earlier generation to crucify Jesus, he presents every conceivable argument why their successors should now accept Jesus as the promised Messiah.

To many of us today, the form of this advocacy doubtless seems alien and out-of-date. Jewish minds may immediately appreciate its power, and pick up without effort the subtler points in Matthew's case: most readers have to learn in patient detail how wonderfully relevant Matthew's arguments are to the thought and circumstances of his time. For all that, Matthew's statement of the case for Christianity in Jewish terms has implications that are universal and timeless.

For example: Matthew's insistence upon Christ's fulfilment of scriptural foregleams and prophetic promises enshrines the truth that in Jesus 'something momentous is going forward', both in the unfolding of God's purpose for mankind and in the attainment of the age-old longings of the human heart. The fulfilment, when it came, outshone both promise and expectation, so that Christianity in the end broke with Judaism altogether; yet all that was true and valuable in Jewish inheritance is conserved in Christ for a wider world.

Thus the mission of Jesus perfects the mission of the former Israel and extends through the new Israel—the new tenants of God's vineyard, the hitherto uninvited guests at Messiah's banquet— to the church among the Gentiles, the followers of Messiah among all nations, to the end of the age. Matthew says nothing of a failure and a fresh beginning: it is one divine movement in history from Abraham and David through Christ to the present, and on to the end-time, a movement initiated and sustained by God, who finds *his people* where he will, according to their faith. The invitation to share that ongoing initiative of God still stands, for Jews as for Gentiles.

Inevitably, such a view of divine activity involved the adjustment of merely nationalistic hopes and the rejection of one who resolutely refused to be what popular expectation demanded. Turning from the temptation to found his kingdom by bribe, miracle, or political expediency, and from the axe, flail and fire of John's prefiguring, Jesus offered a messiahship that healed the sick, the lame, the deaf, that brought good news to the poor, that found in the Servant who would not strive or cry, the king upon a donkey, its definitive expression. Though authoritative in word and powerful in deed, he yet bore the sickness and the sin of many—meek in heart, and humiliated among men. Possibly this is the meaning of the strange question about whose son Messiah is, remembering that in Hebrew 'sonship' signifies similarity. For Jesus was *not* in any ethical or religious sense a son of the all-conquering, giant-killing, militarily expansionist David, but the humble servant of God and man, who came not to be served but to serve.

With this re-interpretation of messiahship is involved a transvaluation of all ideas of greatness, majesty, and power. As magnificence and force were not to be his way, so 'it shall not be so among you'. Matthew's 'explanation' of the Jews' rejection of their Messiah is both historically cogent and spiritually challenging *for all time*.

In the same way, Matthew's representation of Christ as the new rabbi, greater than Moses, who with supreme assurance reinterprets God's will and law—concerning the sabbath, adultery, revenge, oaths, divorce, almsgiving, prayer, fasting, ritual cleanness, the great commandment, resurrection, the Temple worship, and the messianic hope— carries universal implications. More is here than a cultural adjustment of ancient codes and a more enlightened casuistry. For Jesus so radicalises the law, so explores the divine intention behind the commandment, so focuses God's will and man's duty into love for God and neighbour, as to dissolve legalism into God-like benevolence, and show for all generations what the kingly Father requires of men.

As for the monstrous outrage, in Jewish eyes, of a Messiah rejected and slain, Matthew's case is again unanswerable, and not for Jews only. The identification of the Messiah with the Servant 'explains' the death of Jesus, at least as foreseen, foretold, and divinely intended, with all the authority of Isaiah. So does the identification of the Messiah with the Shepherd of Israel, as smitten in defending the sheep, and as enthroned to divide the sheep from the goats. This conception reaches back through Ezekiel and David—king among shepherds—to the shepherd-kings of patriarchal times. In it, the perils of the shepherd's calling and the self-denial of the shepherd's devotion bring their own light to Calvary, for all men.

Clearest of all is the way that Matthew recounts the story of the cross for Jewish ears, by letting the Christ himself interpret the meaning of the event. Fourteen times Jesus speaks in *Matthew* 26–28, and it requires no ingenuity to distil from his utterances the significance that he himself—and so Matthew—found in his death. In these sayings, Jesus twice links his passion with the Passover festival that celebrated Israel's earlier experience of redemptive liberation. Seven times reference is made to God's will or purpose, or to the constraint of scripture; though, on the one hand, Jesus' own voluntary surrender to that will is dramatically emphasised, as in Gethsemane—God's will is not imposed upon Christ; on the other hand, his betrayal remains the fully responsible and culpable act of a wicked man, which must meet judgement.

Central to Matthew's interpretation of the cross are Jesus' words at the Table, embracing a new covenant, in bread and blood, which achieves forgiveness for sinful men, by the 'pouring out' of his soul unto death; a covenant in which also the promise of eternal fellowship together in the coming kingdom is assured. That further link of his death with his messianic destiny informs also Jesus' answers at his trial, both to the high priest and to Pilate. The closing verse of the Gospel shows why: because the cross is, with all else, the way for Messiah from meekness to authority, from humiliation to majesty and power.

Despite the Jewish language and symbolism, this remains the meaning of the cross for all time and for all men. Behind and through man's base betrayal, and through Jesus' own perfect obedience, there moved the long-prepared purpose of God to re-establish his covenant, through sacrifice and forgiveness, with liberated men. That is why the Christ had to die, passing through death from rejection and meekness to timeless authority and power as 'Lord-designate of the world'. And Matthew's authority for that interpretation is none less than God's own interpreter, lawgiver, saviour and king.

For skill, insight, and eloquence, Matthew is no mean advocate of the faith he defends.

The mind of the pastor

Nevertheless, it is as a pastor that Matthew emerges most clearly from his book. Pastoral care is evident in his recalling of Christ's counsel on day-to-day problems of discipleship in the early years of church life: on Christian marriage, on the right use of the sabbath, on fasting and uncleanness, on exorcisms, on the church's attitude towards children, on the payment of taxes and Temple dues. Matthew's pastoral concern lends warmth to his words about caring for, not 'offending', not despising, the 'little ones' who believe; and about caring for, going after, welcoming back and forgiving, the erring ones.

Matthew's wider church responsibilities make him recall the strong words of Jesus about unity and brotherliness; and about the nature, founding, function, worship, work, and future, of the church, as sharing fully Christ's mission in the world, his authority, his rejection, his vindication, and his divine reward. Experience and realism make Matthew aware of the mixed character of the church, and sharpen his constant warning of a judgement, a settling of accounts, that will sort out good from bad, true from false. Self-deception is therefore perilous: the urgent need is that those 'ostensibly disciples' shall be sure where they stand, with Christ or against him, for God or mammon, on the way to life or to destruction.

That warning stems from one of the three main pastoral themes of Matthew: his recalling of Jesus' demand for righteousness exceeding that of the scribes and Pharisees. In the Sermon, in the parables, and in many separate sayings, Jesus calls for specific obedience to the will of the Father, observance of the Father's law as he defines it. He requires the obedience of sons whose spoken profession of loyalty matters less than their actual deeds; the wisdom which, by carefully building upon what he says, proves more important in the storms of life than merely knowing what he taught.

Matthew is *the* textbook of Christ's ethic precisely because in it Christ's interpretation of the will of the Father is fully set out, and nothing at all is accepted —neither profession of Christ as Lord, nor the possession of spiritual gifts, nor a record of public service, nor anything else—as a substitute for obedience.

Matthew's recall of Jesus' words about the advent-hope is likewise pastorally motivated. He knows the disappointment, and the scepticism, bred by the delay of the Lord's coming—and their spiritual effects in the life of the church. Matthew *accepts* the delay, as a fact to be reckoned with, and plays down eschatological excitement: 'the end is not yet'. But the advent is certain, all the same. It is as necessary to the full revelation of the glory of Christ as it is to the completion of his work and the fulfilment of his destiny. Uncertainty about the time and manner of the coming is but a spur to vigilance, as faithfulness, service, and love, are the only fitting ways of making ready for the arriving Lord. Matthew plainly understands the moods and motives of his fellow-members, weary of long endurance and disheartened by delayed promises.

A pastor's mind is evident again in Matthew's assessment of the church's continuing powerlessness in face of the world's ills: its demonic evil, its storms of persecution, its hungry hordes; and in the diagnosis of the cause, the 'little-faith' of believers in their mighty, miracle-working Lord, ever present in the midst of the congregation. Hence the 'eight stories, one phrase used five times, another four times, and other instances all saying first negatively and then positively that the secret of power is faith'—an active, energetic, obstacle-overcoming faith expressed in deeds not feelings, and focused on the Christ who (in Matthew's representation) is deliberately moved to the centre of every story of power. The faith that releases energy within the church enabling her to survive the world's opposition and to serve the world's need, is faith in the risen, wonder-working Christ in the midst of 'the two or three' and with us to the end of the age.

Such focusing upon Christ is of course the distinguishing mark of all truly Christian pastoral work. Matthew offers neither a treatise on morals, an epistle of exhortation, nor an apocalypse warning of doom. His mind is fashioned by and devoted to the story, the teaching, the example, the obedience and the faith of Christ: he chooses the Gospel-form precisely because he would face the congregation again with the figure of Jesus, in meekness and majesty, in humiliation and power, expounding the law of God and revealing his love, passing from rejection through death to glory, belonging equally to his life-time, the church-time and the end-time, the Christ on earth, ascended, and coming, in whom alone the church and the world may find hope.

In the last resort, all Matthew writes is directed towards improving individual discipleship, the discipleship that is childlike in humility, heroic in endurance, one which understands Christ and follows him; the discipleship that knows the teaching and does the will of its Lord, renouncing all that hinders in the search for the kingdom of God and his righteousness. The right temper of the disciple is that of the learner, the child, the earnest servant, for he may never forget that he is on probation, with a sixfold reminder of the possibility of being repudiated at the last; only he that endures to the end shall be saved.

Yet the disciple need not fear, as the church need not fail, for the risen Lord is always with us. The ringing, challenging, yet triumphant last words of Jesus on earth comprise in one declaration the world-wide mission, limitless power, and perpetual Presence that is the secret of the church's invincible perseverance. Beyond that even Matthew, advocate, pastor, and scribe well-trained in the kingdom of God, has nothing further to say.